Introduction

Quiltmaking can be an enjoyable and lifelong hobby. A few of the things that make it so are the number of unique blocks that can be incorporated into a quilt along with the various techniques used to make quilt blocks. There's always something new and exciting to try.

For a new or novice quilter, some quilting techniques can be challenging. But they don't have to be! A good source for learning the techniques is key. We have combined many of the different basic techniques into a unique sampler quilt so you can learn as you make each quilt block. We have included instructions for Sew & Flip Corners, Half- and Quarter-Square Triangles, 4-at-a-Time Flying Geese, Partial Seams and Square-in-a-Square techniques. As you progress through the quilt, the blocks will become a little more challenging, allowing you to improve on your newly learned skills.

In addition, there will be tips along the way and three bonus projects at the end.

Enjoy the journey!

Table of Contents

Daydream Sampler

Design by Carolyn Beam
Quilted by Donna Smith

Fabric Requirements

Skill Level

Confident Beginner

Finished Sizes

Quilt Size: 68" x 87"
Block Size: 16" x 16"
Number of Blocks: 12

Project Notes

Read all instructions before beginning this project.

Cutting lists are given in individual block chapters, except where noted.

Stitch right sides together using a ¼" seam allowance unless otherwise specified.

Materials and cutting lists assume 40" of usable fabric width for yardage.

WOF – width of fabric
HST – half-square triangle ⧅
QST – quarter-square triangle ⊠

Materials

Materials listed are for complete quilt.

- ¼ yard each white print #4 and blue print #1*
- ⅓ yard yellow print #3*
- ⅜ yard each yellow print #1, green print #1, gray prints #2–#4 and white print #2*
- ½ yard each white print #1, blue prints #2 and #3, and gray print #1*
- ⅝ yard each green prints #2 and #3*
- ¾ yard yellow print #2*
- 1¾ yards each white #3 and blue print #4*
- 2¼ yards gray print #5*
- ⅞ yard multicolored stripe*
- 5⅓ yards backing*
- 76" x 95" batting*
- Thread
- Template material
- Fabric marking pencil
- Basic sewing tools and supplies

**Fabrics from the Spring Brook collection by Corey Yoder for Moda Fabrics and Warm & Natural batting from The Warm Company used to make sample.*

Here's a Tip

Cut a small square from each fabric and tape it to a piece of paper, numbering each fabric. Keep this as a handy guide and refer to it and the provided Daydream Fabric Chart as you cut your fabrics and make your blocks. Not all fabrics are used in every block.

Here's a Tip

Pressing

Before pressing seams to one side or open, lay the iron on top of the seam just as it was sewn to set the seam. In quilting, seams are generally pressed toward the darker fabric to avoid shadows on the lighter fabric. If multiple seams come together, it's OK to press them open to distribute the bulk and make it easier to quilt.

Daydream Fabric Chart

FABRICS FROM THE SPRING BROOK COLLECTION BY COREY YODER FOR MODA FABRICS

BLUE #1

BLUE #2

BLUE #3

BLUE #4

GRAY #1

GRAY #2

GRAY #3

GRAY #4

GRAY #5

YELLOW #1

YELLOW #2

YELLOW #3

GREEN #1

GREEN #2

GREEN #3

WHITE #1

WHITE #2

WHITE #3

WHITE #4

MULTICOLORED STRIPE

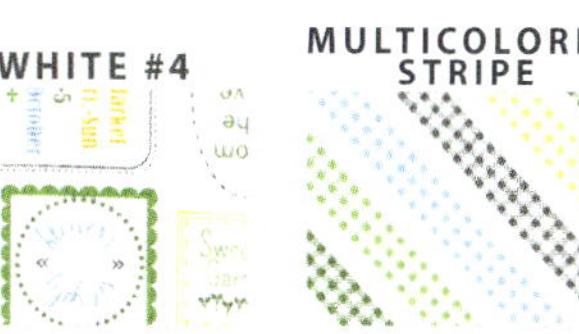

Here's a Tip

Leaders–Enders

Keep an assortment of light and dark 2½" squares handy. Sew a light and dark square together at the beginning of each chain piecing set as your "leader." When you finish your chain piecing, sew another set of squares together as your "ender." Leave your "ender" in your sewing machine and it will become your "leader" for your next set of chain piecing. Using leaders and enders is a way to save thread, eliminate long thread tails at the beginning and ending of your sewing, and prevent thread from bunching up under your sewing. When you have a collection of two square units, sew them together into four-patches. This is a great way to start a scrappy quilt.

CHAPTER 1

Accurate Seam Allowance

Log Cabin

Work with straight strips and practice accurate seam allowances.

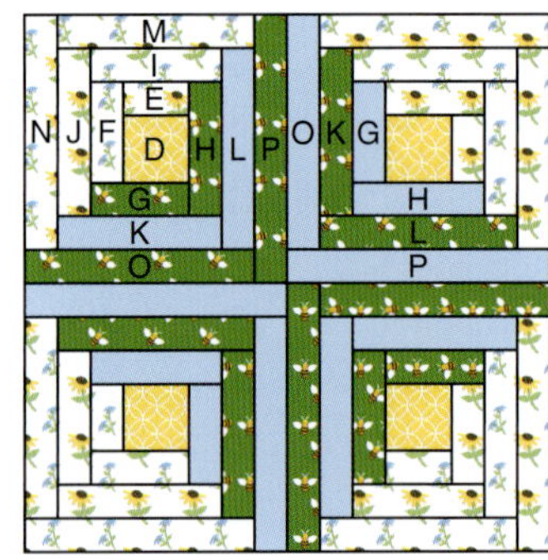

Log Cabin
16" x 16" Finished Block
Make 1

Cutting

From blue print #2 cut:

- 2 (1½" x WOF) strips, then subcut into:
  - 2 (1½" x 3½") G strips
  - 2 (1½" x 4½") H strips
  - 2 (1½" x 5½") K strips
  - 2 (1½" x 6½") L strips
  - 2 (1½" x 7½") O strips
  - 2 (1½" x 8½") P strips

From yellow print #1 cut:

- 4 (2½") D squares

From green print #3 cut:

- 2 (1½" x WOF) strips, then subcut into:
  - 2 (1½" x 3½") G strips
  - 2 (1½" x 4½") H strips
  - 2 (1½" x 5½") K strips
  - 2 (1½" x 6½") L strips
  - 2 (1½" x 7½") O strips
  - 2 (1½" x 8½") P strips

From white print #1 cut:

- 4 (1½" x WOF) strips, then subcut into:
  - 4 (1½" x 2½") E strips
  - 4 (1½" x 3½") F strips
  - 4 (1½" x 4½") I strips
  - 4 (1½" x 5½") J strips
  - 4 (1½" x 6½") M strips
  - 4 (1½" x 7½") N strips

Completing the Block

1. Referring to Figure 1, stitch an E strip to the top of a D square as shown. Press. Stitch an F strip to the left side of the E-D unit. Press.

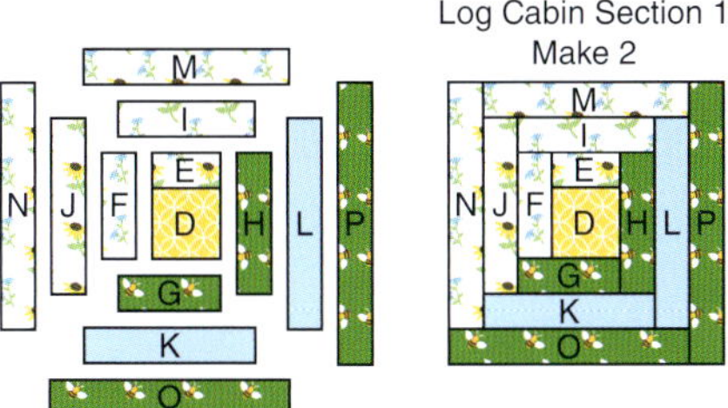

Figure 1

2. Referring again to Figure 1, continue adding strips counterclockwise in alphabetical order using one each green print #3 G, H, O and P strip, one each blue print #2 K and L strip, and one each I, J, M and N strip to complete log cabin section 1. Make two.

3. Referring to Figure 2, stitch an E strip to the right side of a D square. Press. Stitch an F strip to the top. Press.

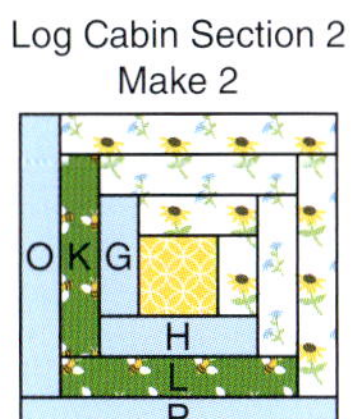

Figure 2

Here's a Tip

Checking Seam Allowance

An accurate ¼" seam allowance is essential for quilting. To test your seam allowance, sew two 2½" squares together. This unit should measure 2½" x 4½". If it measures less than 4½", try sewing with a "scant" ¼" seam, meaning sew the two squares together with a seam allowance slightly (a thread width) less than ¼". You can also lay a strip of tape on your sewing machine bed as a guide or adjust your sewing machine needle until you can sew an accurate ¼" seam.

4. Continue adding strips counterclockwise in alphabetical order using one each blue print #2 G, H, O and P strip, one each green print #3 K and L strip, and one each I, J, M and N strip to complete a log cabin section 2. Make two.

5. Refer to the Log Cabin block diagram to arrange sections 1 and sections 2 in two rows. Sew the sections into rows; sew the rows together. Press.

CHAPTER 2

Sew & Flip Corners

Split Rail

Learn the Sew & Flip Corners technique.

Split Rail
16" x 16" Finished Block
Make 1

Cutting

From green print #1 cut:

- 2 (1½" x WOF) strips

From yellow print #3 cut:

- 2 (1½" x WOF) strips

From blue print #3 cut:

- 2 (1½" x WOF) strips

From gray print #4 cut:

- 2 (1½" x WOF) strips

From gray print #3 cut:

- 20 (2½") A squares

Completing the Block

1. Stitch one 1½" x WOF strip each green print #1, yellow print #3, blue print #3 and gray print #4 together along the length to make a strip set as shown in Figure 1. Make two. Cut strip sets into 16 (4½"-wide) segments.

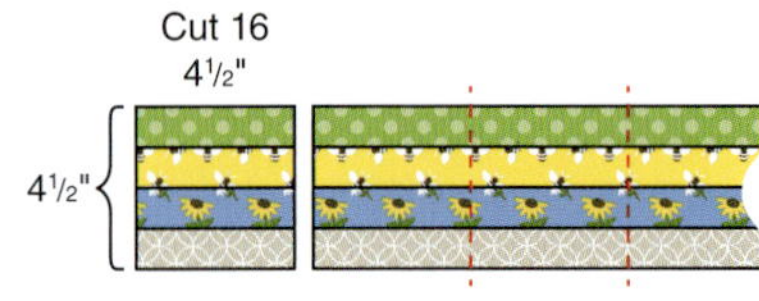

Figure 1

2. Referring to Sew & Flip Corners, sew one A square to the blue/gray corner of a step 1 segment as shown in Figure 2, paying attention to the orientation of the segment strips, to make unit 1. Make 10.

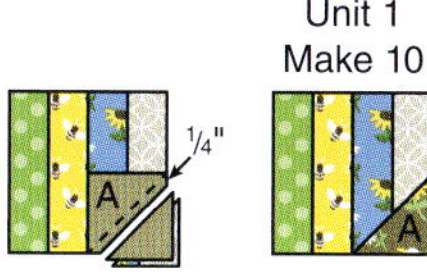

Figure 2

3. Repeat, placing A square on a green/yellow corner, to make six of unit 2 as shown in Figure 3, noting position of the A square and orientation of the segment strips.

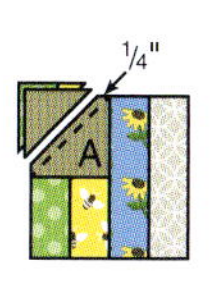

Figure 3

4. In the same manner, make four of unit 3 by adding a second A square to the opposite corner of a unit 1 as shown in Figure 4.

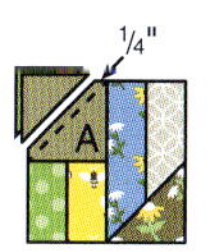

Figure 4

5. Referring to the Split Rail block diagram, arrange the units into four rows. Join the units in each row; press. Sew the rows together. Press.

SEW & FLIP CORNERS

Use this method to add triangle corners in a quilt block.

1. Draw a diagonal line from corner to corner on the wrong side of the specified square. Place the square, right sides together, on the indicated corner of the larger piece, making sure the line is oriented in the correct direction indicated by the pattern (Figure 1).

2. Sew on the drawn line. Trim ¼" away from sewn line (Figure 2).

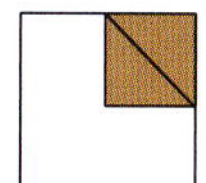

Figure 1

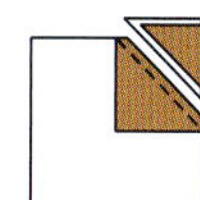

Figure 2

3. Open and press to reveal the corner triangle (Figure 3).

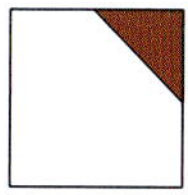

Figure 3

4. If desired, square up the finished unit to the required unfinished size. ●

CHAPTER 3

Sew & Flip Corners

Bow Tie

Practice the Sew & Flip Corners technique.

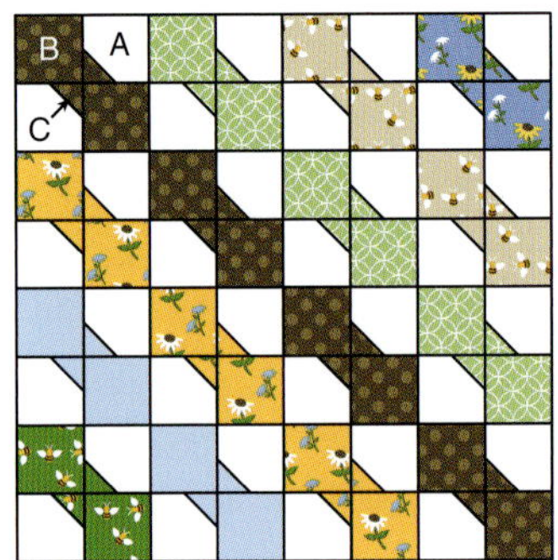

Bow Tie
16" x 16" Finished Block
Make 1

Cutting

From blue print #1 cut:

- 4 (2½") B squares
- 4 (1½") C squares

From blue print #3 cut:

- 2 (2½") B squares
- 2 (1½") C squares

From green print #2 cut:

- 6 (2½") B squares
- 6 (1½") C squares

From green print #3 cut:

- 2 (2½") B squares
- 2 (1½") C squares

From gray print #1 cut:

- 8 (2½") B squares
- 8 (1½") C squares

From gray print #2 cut:

- 4 (2½") B squares
- 4 (1½") C squares

From yellow print #2 cut:

- 6 (2½") B squares
- 6 (1½") C squares

From white #3 cut:

- 32 (2½") A squares

Completing the Block

1. Referring to Sew & Flip Corners on page 7, use A squares and C squares to make 32 A-C units in the quantities shown, referring to Figure 1.

- 8 gray print #1
- 6 each yellow print #2 and green print #2
- 4 each blue print #1 and gray print #2
- 2 each blue print #3 and green print #3

A-C Units
Make 32 total

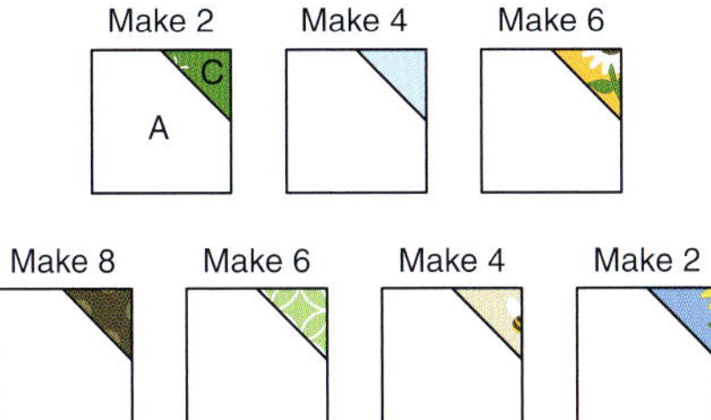

Figure 1

2. Arrange two matching A-C units and B squares as shown in Figure 2. Sew together in rows; join the rows to make one bow tie unit. Make 16.

Figure 2

3. Referring to the Bow Tie block diagram, arrange the bow tie units into four rows. Stitch the units into rows; press. Stitch the rows together; press.

CHAPTER 4

Sew & Flip Corners

Arkansas Crossroads

Practice the Sew & Flip Corners technique.

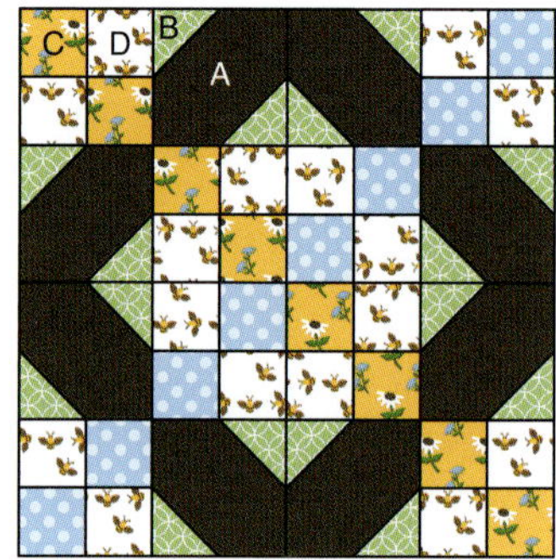

Arkansas Crossroads
16" x 16" Finished Block
Make 1

Cutting

From gray print #5 cut:

- 8 (4½") A squares

From green print #2 cut:

- 16 (2½") B squares

From blue print #2 cut:

- 8 (2½") C squares

From yellow print #2 cut:

- 8 (2½") C squares

From white print #2 cut:

- 16 (2½") D squares

Completing the Block

1. Referring to Sew & Flip Corners on page 7, use A squares and B squares to make eight A-B units as shown in Figure 1.

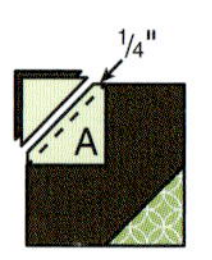

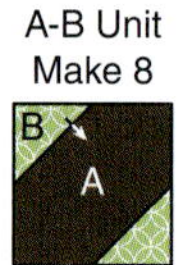

Figure 1

2. Stitch a blue print #2 C square and a D square together as shown in Figure 2. Make eight blue C-D units. Stitch two blue C-D units together to make a four-patch. Make four blue four-patch units.

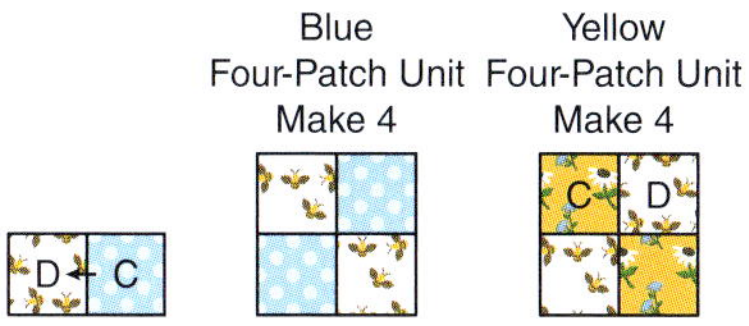

Blue
Four-Patch Unit
Make 4

Yellow
Four-Patch Unit
Make 4

C D

Figure 2

3. Repeat, referring again to Figure 2, to make four yellow four-patch units as shown.

4. Refer to the Arkansas Crossroads block diagram to arrange the units into four rows. Stitch the units into rows; sew the rows together to complete the Arkansas Crossroads block.

CHAPTER 5

Half-Square Triangles

Basket

Learn to make half-square triangles.

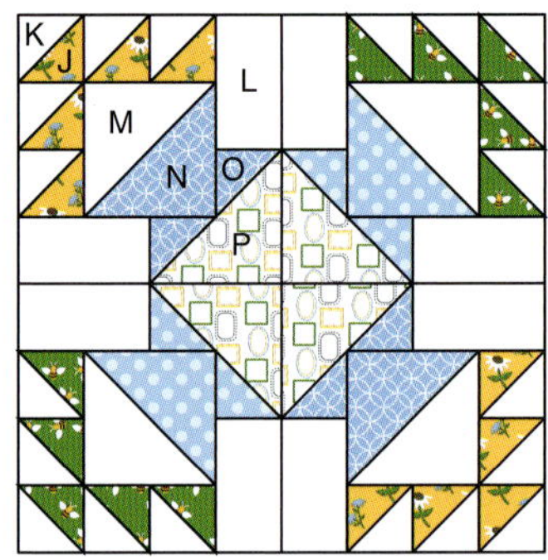

Basket
16" x 16" Finished Block
Make 1

Cutting

From yellow print #2 cut:

- 5 (3") J squares

From green print #3 cut:

- 5 (3") J squares

From white #3 cut:

- 10 (3") K squares
- 8 (2½" x 4½") L rectangles
- 2 (5") M squares

From blue print #2 cut:

- 1 (5") N square
- 2 (2⅞") O squares, then cut once diagonally ⧅

From blue print #4 cut:

- 1 (5") N square
- 2 (2⅞") O squares, then cut once diagonally ⧅

From white print #4 cut:

- 2 (4⅞") P squares, then cut once diagonally ⧅

Completing the Block

1. Referring to Half-Square Triangles, use K squares and yellow print #2 J squares to make 10 yellow J-K units as shown in Figure 1. Trim each unit to 2½" square, keeping seam centered.

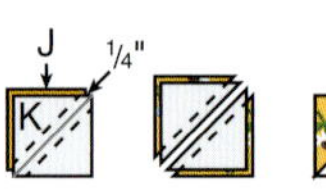

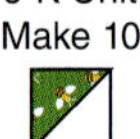

Figure 1

2. Repeat to make 10 green J-K units as shown in Figure 1.

3. In the same manner, make two blue #2 M-N units and two blue #4 M-N units as shown in Figure 2. Trim each unit to 4½", keeping seam centered.

Blue #2 M-N Unit Make 2

Blue #4 M-N Unit Make 2

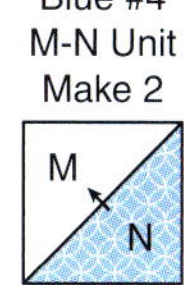

Figure 2

4. Referring to Figure 3, stitch two yellow J-K units together as shown. Stitch to the side of a blue #4 M-N unit. Stitch three yellow J-K units together and stitch to the top as shown.

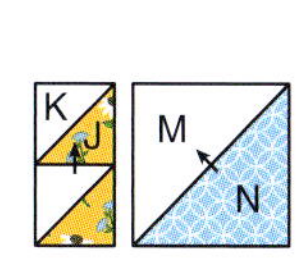

Figure 3

5. Stitch blue print #4 O triangles to two L rectangles as shown in Figure 4. Stitch L-O units to adjacent sides of the step 4 unit as shown. Stitch a P triangle to the corner to complete a yellow basket unit. Make two.

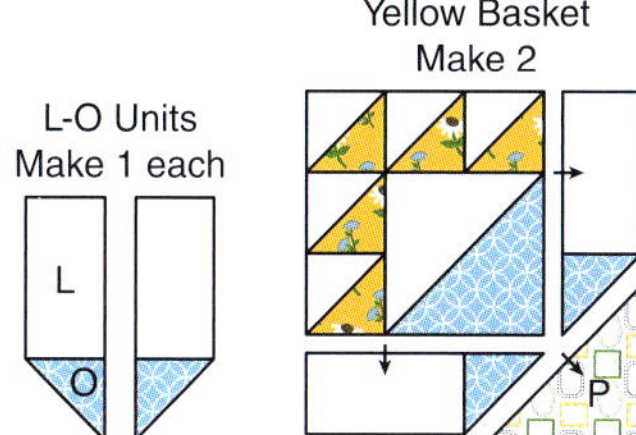

Figure 4

6. Repeat steps 4 and 5 using the green J-K units, blue #2 M-N units, blue print #2 O triangles, L rectangles and a P triangle to make two green basket units as shown in Figure 5.

Green Basket
Make 2

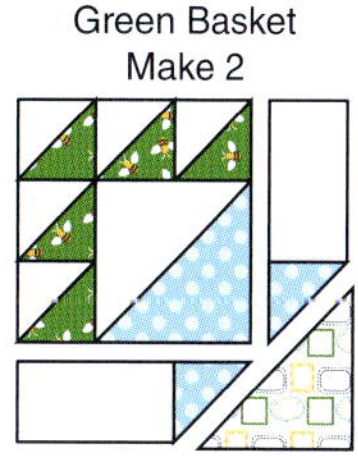

Figure 5

7. Referring to the Basket block diagram, arrange the basket units in two rows. Sew into rows; sew the rows together to complete the Basket block.

HALF-SQUARE TRIANGLES

Half-square triangles (HSTs) are a basic unit of quilting used in many blocks or on their own. This construction method will yield two HSTs.

1. Refer to the pattern for size to cut squares. The standard formula is to add ⅞" to the finished size of the square. Cut two squares from different colors this size. For example, for a 3" finished HST unit, cut 3⅞" squares.

2. Draw a diagonal line from corner to corner on the wrong side of the lightest color square. Layer the squares right sides together. Stitch ¼" on either side of the drawn line (Figure A).

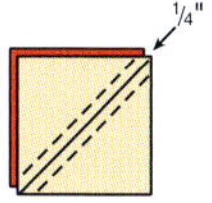

Figure A

3. Cut the squares apart on the drawn line, leaving a ¼" seam allowance and making two HST units referring to Figure B.

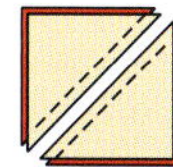

Figure B

4. Open the HST units and press seam allowances toward the darker fabric making two HST units (Figure C). ●

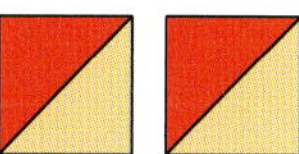

Figure C

CHAPTER 6

Quarter-Square Triangles

Square & Star

Learn to make quarter-square triangles.

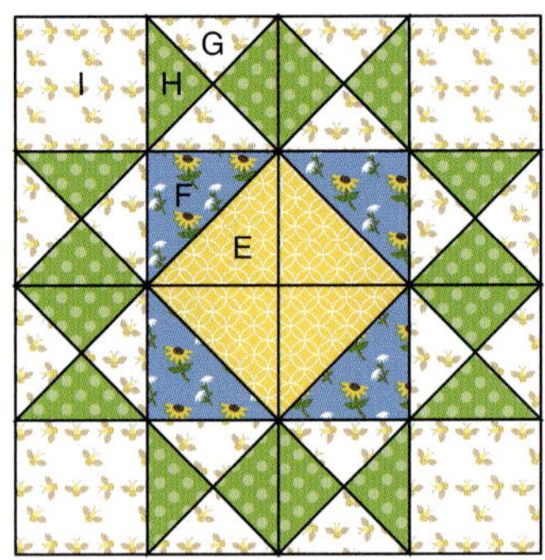

Square & Star
16" x 16" Finished Block
Make 1

Cutting

From yellow print #1 cut:

- 2 (5") E squares

From blue print #3 cut:

- 2 (5") F squares

From white print #2 cut:

- 4 (5½") G squares
- 4 (4½") I squares

From green print #1 cut:

- 4 (5½") H squares

Completing the Block

1. Referring to Half-Square Triangles on page 13, use E squares and F squares to make four E-F units as shown in Figure 1. Trim each unit to 4½" square, keeping seam centered.

Figure 1

2. In the same manner, make eight G-H units as shown in Figure 2.

Figure 2

3. Referring to Quarter-Square Triangles, make eight G-H QST units from step 2 G-H units as shown in Figure 3. Trim QST units to 4½", keeping seam intersection centered.

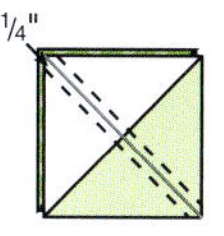

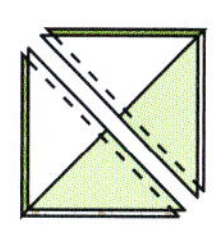

Figure 3

4. Referring to the Square & Star block diagram, arrange the step 1 and step 3 units along with the I squares in four rows. Stitch the units and squares into rows; sew the rows together to complete the Square & Star block.

QUARTER-SQUARE TRIANGLES

Quarter-square triangles (QSTs) are a basic unit of quilting used in many blocks or on their own. This construction method will yield two QST units.

1. Refer to the pattern for size to cut squares. The standard formula is to add 1¼" to the finished size of the square. Cut two squares from different colors this size. For example, for a 3" finished QST unit, cut 4¼" squares.

2. Draw a diagonal line from corner to corner on the wrong side of the lightest color square. Layer the squares right sides together. Stitch ¼" on either side of the drawn line. Cut apart on the drawn line to yield two half-square triangle (HST) units. Open and press toward the darker fabric (Figure A).

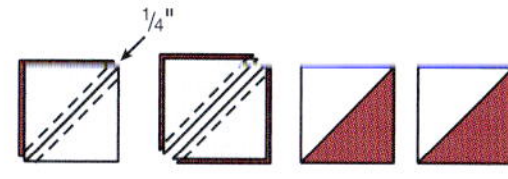

Figure A

3. Draw a diagonal line from corner to corner on the wrong side of one HST unit perpendicular to the seam line (Figure B). Place the two HST units right sides together with opposite colors facing one another. Stitch ¼" on either side of the drawn line.

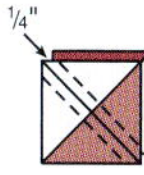

Figure B

4. Cut apart on the drawn line, leaving a ¼" seam allowance and making two QST units (Figure C).

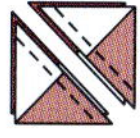

Figure C

5. Open and press to complete two QST units, also known as hourglass units when made of two contrasting fabrics (Figure D). ●

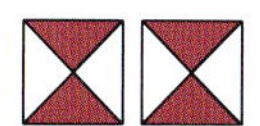

Figure D

CHAPTER 7

Half-Square Triangles and Triangle Combination

Sparkling Star

Add triangles to half-square triangle units to make the larger ones sparkle in this block.

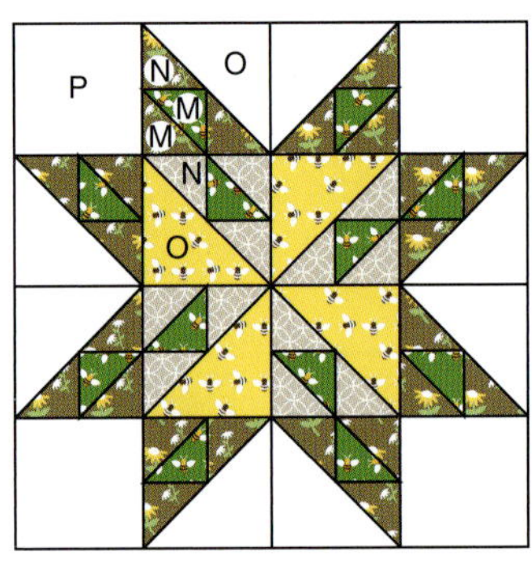

Sparkling Star
16" x 16" Finished Block
Make 1

Cutting

From green print #3 cut:

- 6 (3") M squares

From gray print #3 cut:

- 4 (3") M squares
- 8 (2⅞") N squares, then cut once diagonally ⧅

From gray print #4 cut:

- 2 (3") M squares
- 4 (2⅞") N squares, then cut once diagonally ⧅

From white #3 cut:

- 4 (4⅞") O squares, then cut once diagonally ⧅
- 4 (4½") P squares

From yellow print #3 cut:

- 2 (4⅞") O squares, then cut once diagonally ⧅

Completing the Block

1. Referring to Half-Square Triangles on page 13, use green print #3 M squares and gray print #3 M squares to make eight HST units as shown in Figure 1. Repeat to make four green print #3 and gray print #4 HST units.

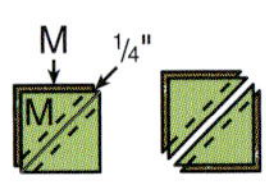

Figure 1

2. Stitch two gray print #3 N triangles to adjacent sides of a gray #3 HST unit to make a gray #3 pieced triangle unit, as shown in Figure 2. Make eight.

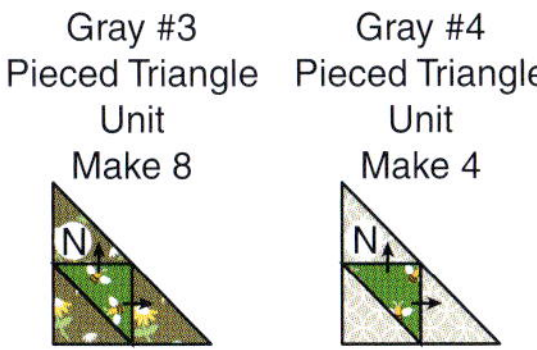

Figure 2

3. Referring again to Figure 2, repeat using gray print #4 N triangles and gray #4 HST units to make four gray #4 pieced triangle units.

4. Stitch a white O triangle to each gray #3 pieced triangle unit as shown in Figure 3. Stitch a yellow O triangle to each gray #4 pieced triangle unit.

Make 8 Make 4

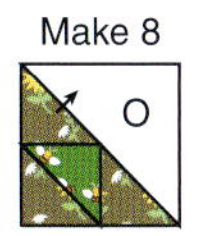

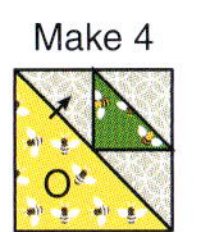

Figure 3

5. Refer to the Sparkling Star block diagram to arrange the units and P squares in four rows. Stitch the pieces in rows; sew the rows together to complete the Sparkling Star block.

CHAPTER 8

Four-at-a-Time Flying Geese and Half-Square Triangles

Fox & Geese

Learn to make four-at-a-time flying geese.

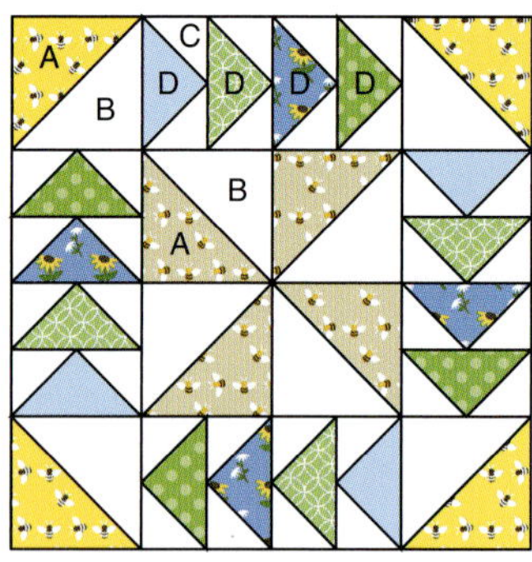

Fox & Geese
16" x 16" Finished Block
Make 1

Cutting

From each of yellow print #3 & gray print #2 cut:

- 2 (5") A squares (4 total)

From white #3 cut:

- 4 (5") B squares
- 16 (2⅞") C squares

From each of blue print #1, blue print #3, green print #1 & green print #2 cut:

- 1 (5¼") D square (4 total)

Completing the Block

1. Referring to Half-Square Triangles on page 13, use yellow print #3 A squares and B squares to make four yellow #3 A-B units as shown in Figure 1. Repeat to make four gray #2 A-B units using gray print #2 A squares and B squares. Trim units to 4½" square, keeping seam centered.

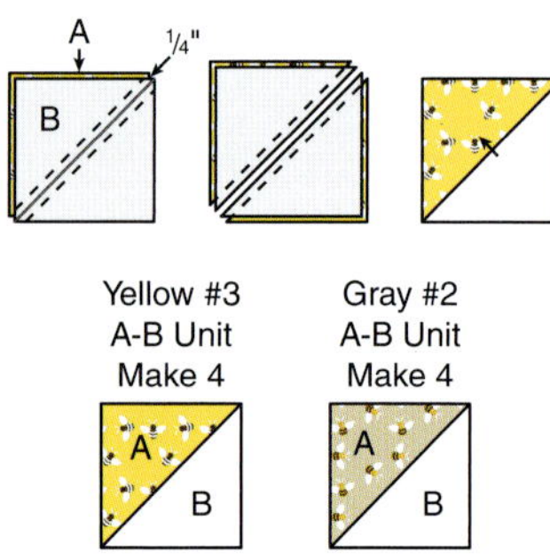

Figure 1

2. Referring to Four-at-a-Time Flying Geese, use C squares and D squares to make four flying geese from each of blue print #1, green print #1, blue print #3 and green print #2 as shown in Figure 2.

Make 4 each

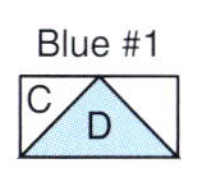

Figure 2

3. Sew one of each color flying geese together as shown in Figure 3. Make a total of four flying geese units.

Figure 3

4. Arrange the four gray #2 A-B units in two rows as shown in Figure 4. Sew units together in rows; join the rows.

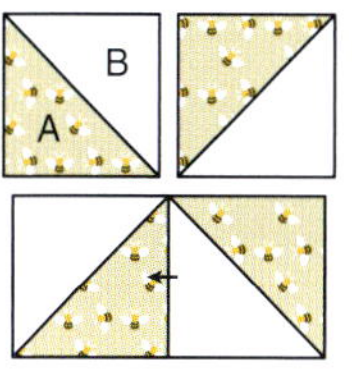

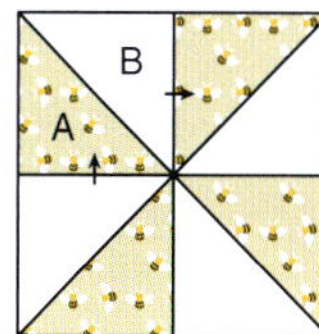

Figure 4

5. Refer to the Fox & Geese block diagram to lay out the units in three rows. Stitch the units into rows; sew the rows together to complete the Fox & Geese block.

FOUR-AT-A-TIME FLYING GEESE

With this method, smaller squares are sewn onto opposite ends of a larger square. The unit is cut in half and additional small squares are sewn on the units. After sewing in place and cutting, the small squares are flipped open to create the flying geese unit.

The large square will be the center of the flying geese units, and the small squares will become the "wings." The bias edges aren't exposed until after sewing, so there is no concern about stretch and distortion (Photo A).

Photo A

Cutting

Refer to the pattern for the sizes to cut the rectangle and squares. Cut as directed in the pattern.

Determine the finished size of the flying geese unit you'd like to make and add 1¼" to the desired finished width of the flying geese unit, then cut one center square.

Add ⅞" to the height of the desired finished flying geese unit and cut four squares.

For example, to make four 2" x 4" finished flying geese units, cut one 5¼" square and four 2⅞" squares.

Assembly

1. Draw a diagonal line on the wrong side of each small square. Orienting the drawn lines as shown in photo, position two small squares on opposite corners of the large square. The small squares will overlap slightly in the middle. Stitch ¼" away from both sides of the marked line. Using a rotary cutter, cut on the marked line to create two units (Photo B).

Photo B

2. Press seam allowances toward the small triangles.

3. Position the remaining squares on the units as shown and stitch ¼" away on each side of the marked line (Photo C).

Photo C

4. Cut on the marked line and press toward the triangles to create a total of four flying geese units (Photo D).

Photo D

5. If desired, trim dog-ears and square up the finished unit to the required unfinished size. ●

CHAPTER 9

Sew & Flip Flying Geese
and Sew & Flip Corners

Tulip

Use the sew-and-flip method to make flying geese and square-in-a-square units.

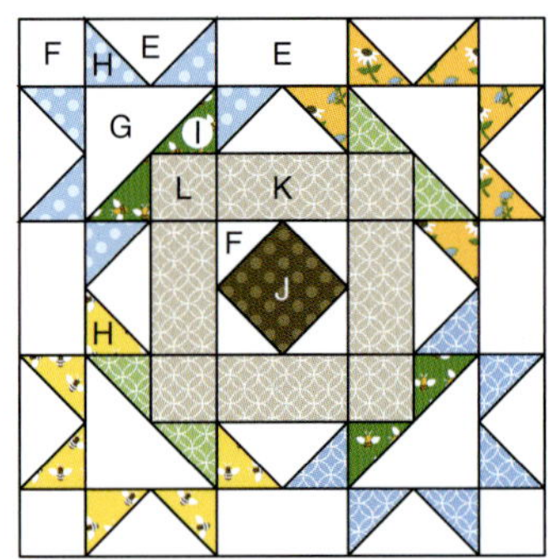

Tulip
16" x 16" Finished Block
Make 1

Cutting

From white #3 cut:

- 2 (4⅞") G squares, then cut once diagonally ◸
- 16 (2½" x 4½") E rectangles
- 8 (2½") F squares

From each of blue print #2, blue print #4, yellow print #2 & yellow print #3 cut:

- 6 (2½") H squares (24 total)

From green print #2 cut:

- 2 (2⅞") I squares, then cut once diagonally ◸

From green print #3 cut:

- 2 (2⅞") I squares, then cut once diagonally ◸

From gray print #1 cut:

- 1 (4½") J square

From gray print #4 cut:

- 4 (2½" x 4½") K rectangles
- 4 (2½") L squares

Completing the Block

1. Referring to Sew & Flip Flying Geese, use blue print #4 H squares and E rectangles to make two blue #4 flying geese units as shown in Figure 1. Repeat to make two flying geese each using yellow print #3, yellow print #2 and blue print #2 H squares as shown.

Flying Geese
Blue #4
Make 2

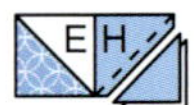

Yellow #3
Make 2

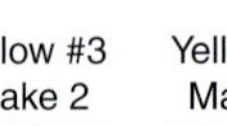

Yellow #2
Make 2

Blue #2
Make 2

H E

Figure 1

2. Repeat to make flying geese units with the remaining H squares in each of the following fabric combinations as shown in Figure 2:

- Blue print #4 and yellow print #3
- Blue print #2 and yellow print #2
- Yellow print #2 and blue print #4
- Yellow print #3 and blue print #2

Blue #4 & yellow #3

Yellow #2 & blue #4

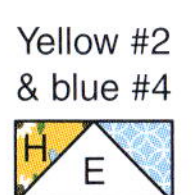

Blue #2 & yellow #2

Yellow #3 & blue #2

Figure 2

3. Stitch matching I triangles to adjacent sides of the L squares to make a triangle unit as shown in Figure 3. Make two triangle units with green print #2 I squares and two with green print #3 I squares.

Figure 3

4. Stitch G triangles to step 3 triangle units as shown in Figure 4.

Make 4 total

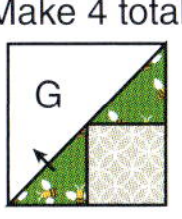

Figure 4

5. Referring to Sew & Flip Corners on page 7, sew F squares on opposite corners of the J square as shown in Figure 5.

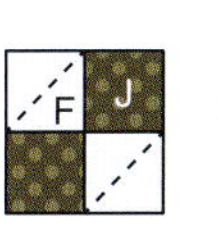

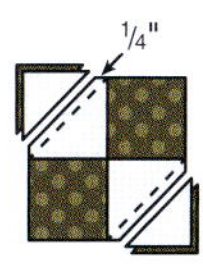

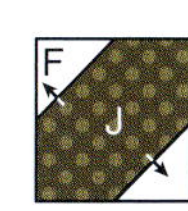

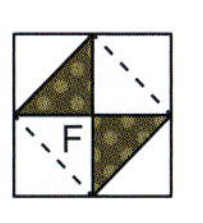

Make 1

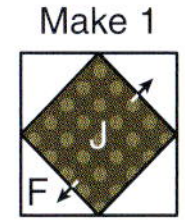

Figure 5

6. Lay out the units from steps 1–5, F squares, and E and K rectangles in five rows as shown in Figure 6, paying careful attention to fabric placement. Stitch the units into rows; sew the rows together to make the Tulip block.

Figure 6

SEW & FLIP FLYING GEESE

With this method, squares are sewn onto opposite ends of a rectangle. The rectangle will be the center of the flying geese unit and the squares will become the "wings." After sewing in place, the squares are trimmed and flipped open to create the unit. The bias edges aren't exposed until after sewing so there is no concern about stretch and distortion.

Cutting

Refer to the pattern for the sizes to cut the rectangle and squares. Cut as directed in the pattern.

Determine the finished size of the flying geese unit you'd like to make and add ½" to the desired finished height and width of the flying geese unit, then cut a rectangle that size.

Cut two squares the same size as the height of the cut rectangle.

For example, to make one 2" x 4" finished flying geese unit, cut a 2½" x 4½" rectangle and two 2½" squares (Photo A).

Photo A

Assembly

1. Draw a diagonal line from corner to corner on the wrong side of each small square.

Place a square, right sides together, on one end of the rectangle. Sew just outside the drawn line (Photo B).

Photo B

2. Using a rotary cutter, trim ¼" away from sewn line.

Open and press to reveal the corner triangle or wing (Photo C).

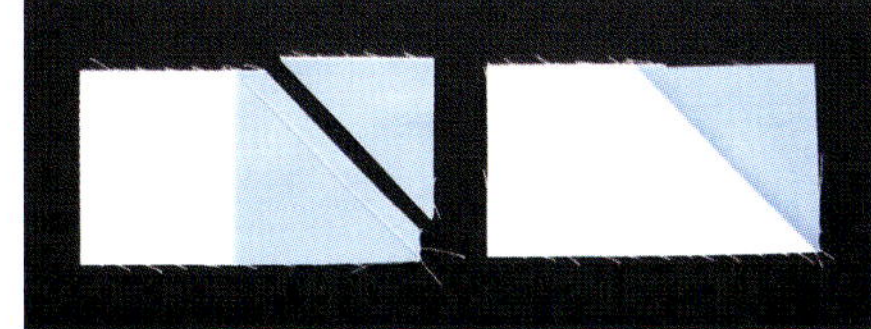

Photo C

3. Place the second square, right sides together, on the opposite end of the rectangle. This square will slightly overlap the previous piece.

Sew just outside the drawn line and trim ¼" away from sewn line as before.

Open and press to complete the flying geese unit (Photo D).

Photo D

4. If desired, square up the finished unit to the required unfinished size. ●

CHAPTER 10

Square-in-a-Square, Sew & Flip Corners, Half-Square Triangles and Four-at-a-Time Flying Geese

Crosses & Losses

Practice making square-in-a-square units, half-square triangles and flying geese.

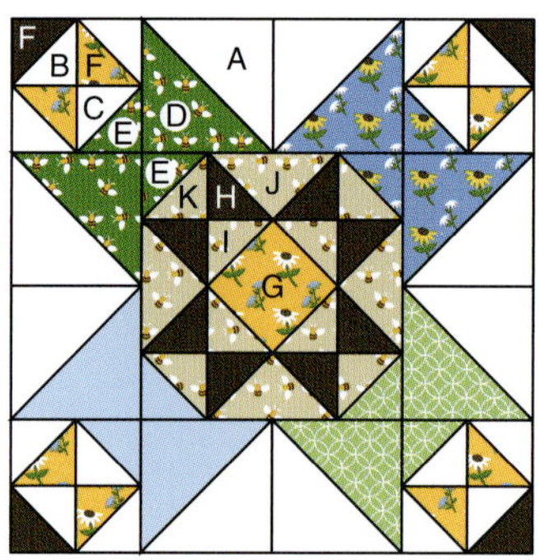

Crosses & Losses
16" x 16" Finished Block
Make 1

Cutting

From white #3 cut:

- 4 (5") A squares
- 6 (3") B squares
- 2 (2⅞") C squares, then cut once diagonally

From each of green print #2, green print #3, blue print #1 and blue print #3 cut:

- 1 (5") D square
- 1 (2⅞") E square, then cut once diagonally

From yellow print #2 cut:

- 4 (3") F squares
- 1 (4½") G square

From gray print #2 cut:

- 1 (5¼") J square
- 2 (2⅞") K squares, then cut once diagonally
- 4 (2½") I squares

From gray print #5 cut:

- 2 (3") F squares
- 4 (2⅞") H squares

Completing the Block

1. Referring to Half-Square Triangles on page 13, use A squares and green print #3 D squares to make two green #3 A-D units as shown in Figure 1. Repeat to make two each blue #1 A-D units, blue #3 A-D units and green #2 A-D units. Trim units to 4½", keeping diagonal seam centered.

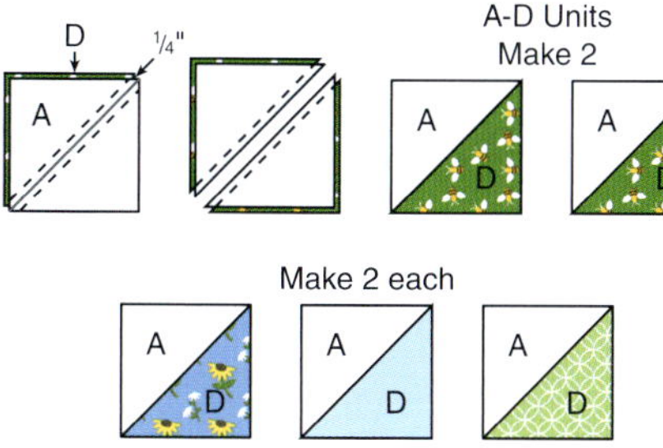

Figure 1

2. Repeat using B squares and gray print #5 F squares to make four gray #5 HSTs and B squares and yellow print #2 F squares to make eight yellow #2 HSTs as shown in Figure 2. Trim units to 2½", keeping diagonal seam centered.

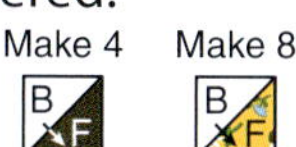

Figure 2

3. Stitch a C HST and a green print #3 E HST together as shown in Figure 3a to make one HST unit. Repeat with blue print #1, blue print #3 and green print #2 E HSTs to make one HST unit of each fabric combination. Trim units to 2½", if necessary, keeping diagonal seam centered.

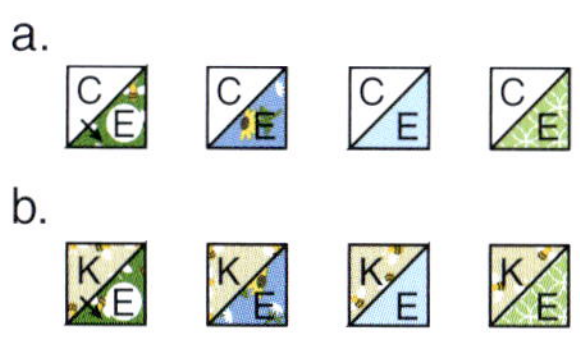

Figure 3

4. Repeat using K HSTs and green print #3, blue print #1, blue print #3 and green print #2 E HSTs as shown in Figure 3b to make one HST of each fabric combination. Trim units to 2½", if necessary, keeping diagonal seam centered.

5. Refer to Sew & Flip Corners on page 7 and sew I squares to corners of a G square as shown in Figure 4.

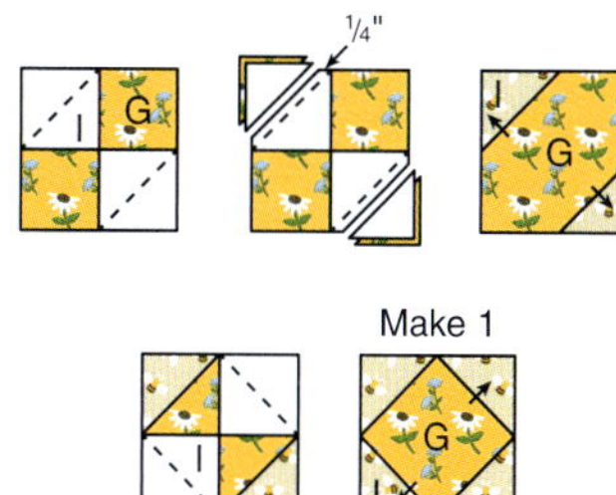

Figure 4

6. Refer to Four-at-a-Time Flying Geese on page 19 and make four flying geese using the H and J squares as shown in Figure 5.

Figure 5

7. Arrange the units from steps 2 and 3 as shown in Figure 6. Sew the units into rows; sew the rows together to make four corner units.

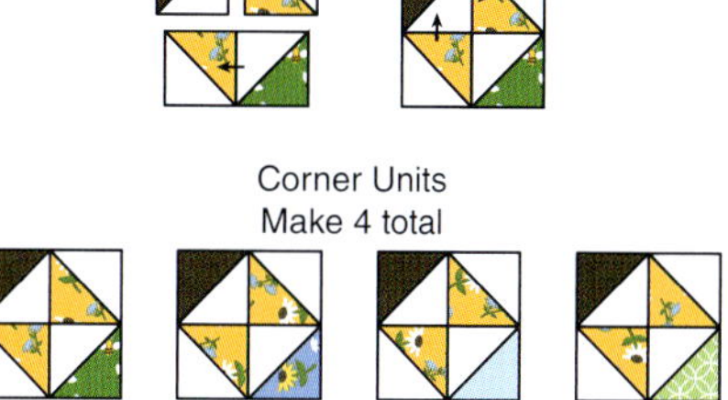

Figure 6

8. Arrange the units from steps 4, 5 and 6 in three rows as shown in Figure 7. Stitch the units into rows; sew the rows together to make the center unit.

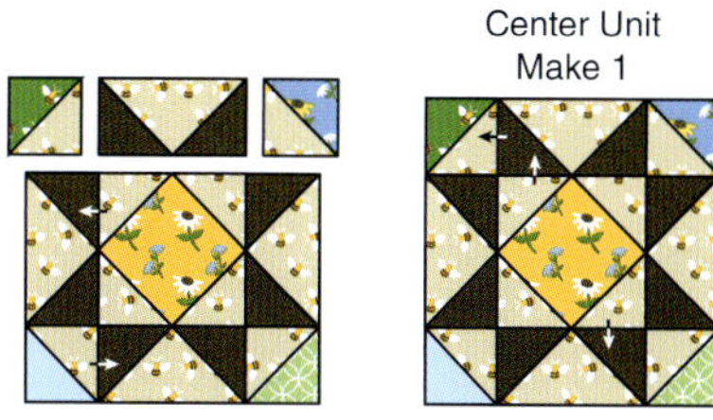

Figure 7

9. Refer to the block diagram to arrange the step 1 units, corner units and center unit into rows, paying close attention to color placement. Stitch the units together into rows; sew the rows together to complete the Crosses & Losses block.

CHAPTER 11

Four-at-a-Time Flying Geese and Half-Square Triangles

Odd Fellows Chain

Practice making four-at-a-time flying geese and half-square triangles.

Odd Fellows Chain
16" x 16" Finished Block
Make 1

Cutting

From white #3 cut:

- 1 (5¼") M square
- 2 (3¾") P squares, then cut once diagonally
- 4 (3") L squares
- 4 (2⅞") O squares, then cut once diagonally
- 8 (2½") N squares

From yellow print #3 cut:

- 4 (3") Q squares

From blue print #1 cut:

- 4 (4⅞") T squares, then cut once diagonally

From gray print #1 cut:

- 1 (4½") R square
- 4 (2⅞") S squares, then cut once diagonally

From white print #1 cut:

- 1 (5¼") M square
- 4 (2½") U squares

From green print #2 cut:

- 4 (2⅞") S squares, then cut once diagonally

Completing the Block

1. Referring to Half-Square Triangles on page 13, use L squares and Q squares to make eight L-Q units as shown in Figure 1. Trim units to 2½", if necessary.

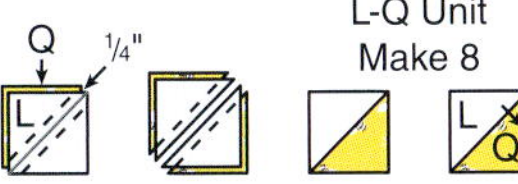

Figure 1

2. Arrange two L-Q units and two N squares into two rows as shown in Figure 2. Sew pieces into rows; sew rows together to make a corner unit. Make four.

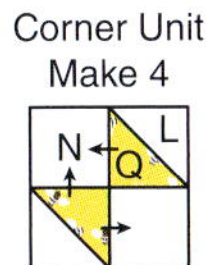

Figure 2

3. Refer to Four-at-a-Time Flying Geese on page 19 and use the white #3 M square and gray print #1 S squares to make four flying geese as shown in Figure 3. Repeat with the white print #1 M square and green print #2 S squares.

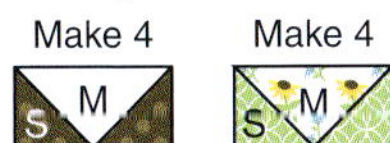

Figure 3

4. Stitch an O triangle to opposite short sides of a gray print #1 flying geese unit as shown in Figure 4. Stitch a P triangle to the bottom. Stitch a T triangle to each side to complete one unit. Make four.

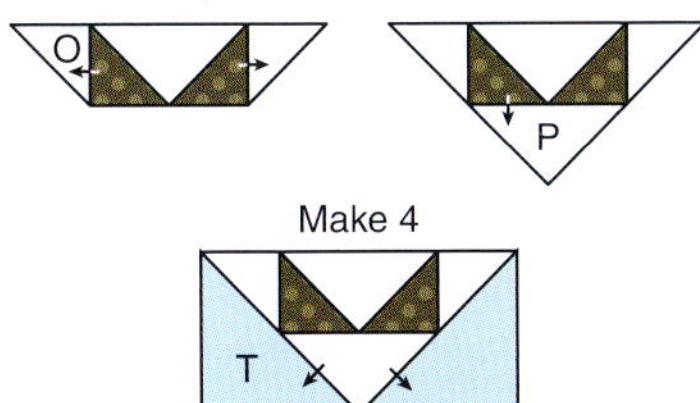

Figure 4

5. Arrange the green print #2 flying geese and the R and U squares in three rows as shown in Figure 5. Stitch the pieces into rows; sew the rows together to make the center star unit.

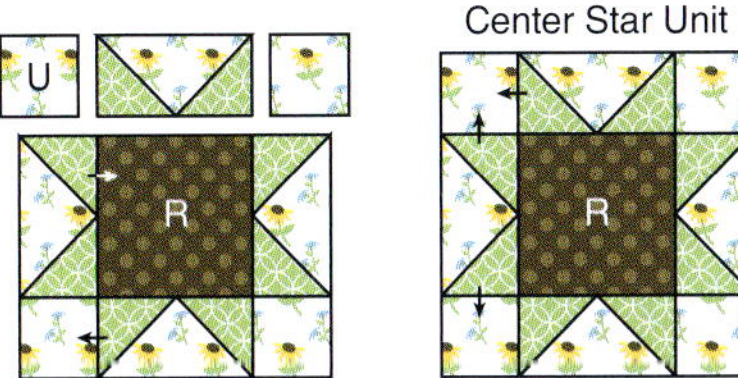

Figure 5

6. Refer to the Odd Fellows Chain block diagram to arrange the corner units, step 4 units and center star in three rows. Stitch the units into rows; sew the rows together to complete the Odd Fellows Chain block.

CHAPTER 12

Using Templates and Partial Seams

Country Village

Use templates and partial seams.

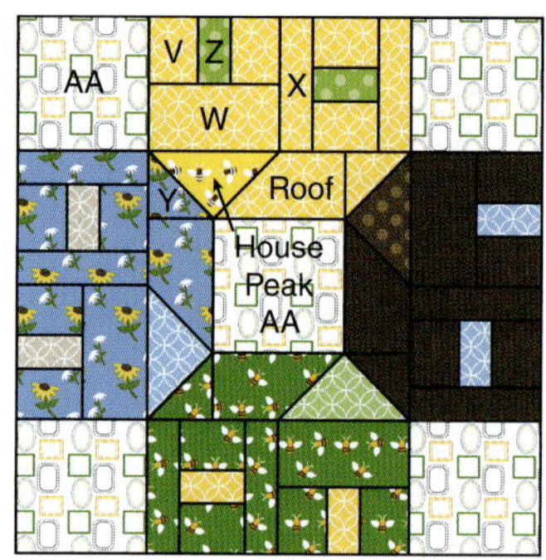

Country Village
16" x 16" Finished Block
Make 1

Cutting

Prepare templates using patterns provided on page 28 for roof and house peak, transferring all markings to templates. Place marked side of template facedown on wrong side of fabric to cut.

From each of green print #3, blue print #3, yellow print #1 and gray print #5 cut:

- 1 (2⅞") Y square, then cut once diagonally (use 1) ⧅
- 1 (2½" x 4½") W rectangle
- 4 (2" x 2½") V rectangles
- 2 (1½" x 4½") X rectangles
- 1 roof shape

From each of yellow print #1, green print #1, gray print #4 and blue print #2 cut:

- 2 (1½" x 2½") Z rectangles

From each of blue print #4, green print #2, yellow print #3 and gray print #1 cut:

- 1 house peak shape

From white print #4 cut:

- 5 (4½") AA squares

Completing the Block

1. Gather the green print #3 V, W, X and Y pieces along with the yellow print #1 Z pieces.

2. Stitch the V rectangles to opposite sides of a Z rectangle as shown in Figure 1. Make two.

Figure 1

3. Stitch an X rectangle to opposite long sides of one step 2 unit as shown in Figure 2a. Stitch a W rectangle to one side of the second step 2 unit as shown in Figure 2b. Stitch the two units together to complete a house unit as shown in Figure 2c. Repeat pairing the blue print #3 and gray print #4 pieces, gray print #5 and blue print #2 pieces, and yellow print #1 and green print #1 pieces as shown.

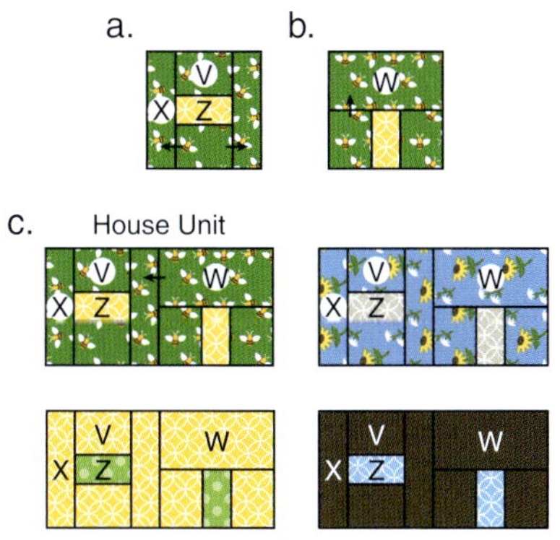

Figure 2

4. Stitch a green print #3 roof, green print #2 house peak and gray print #5 Y triangle together as shown in Figure 3 to make a roof section. Repeat pairing the blue print #3 roof, blue print #4 house peak and green print #3 Y triangle; gray print #5 roof, gray print #1 house peak and yellow print #1 Y triangle; and yellow print #1 roof, yellow print #3 house peak and blue print #3 Y triangle.

Figure 3

5. Referring to Partial Seams on page 28, stitch the green roof section to an AA square using a partial seam and stitching about halfway to the middle of AA as shown in Figure 4. Sew the blue roof to the left, yellow roof to the top and gray roof to the right. Complete the partial seam.

Figure 4

6. Stitch the blue house to the left and gray house to the right to complete the center row as shown in Figure 5.

Figure 5

7. Refer to the block diagram to arrange the remaining AA squares, yellow and green houses, and center row into three rows. Join the pieces and units in the top and bottom rows. Stitch the rows together to complete the Country Village block.

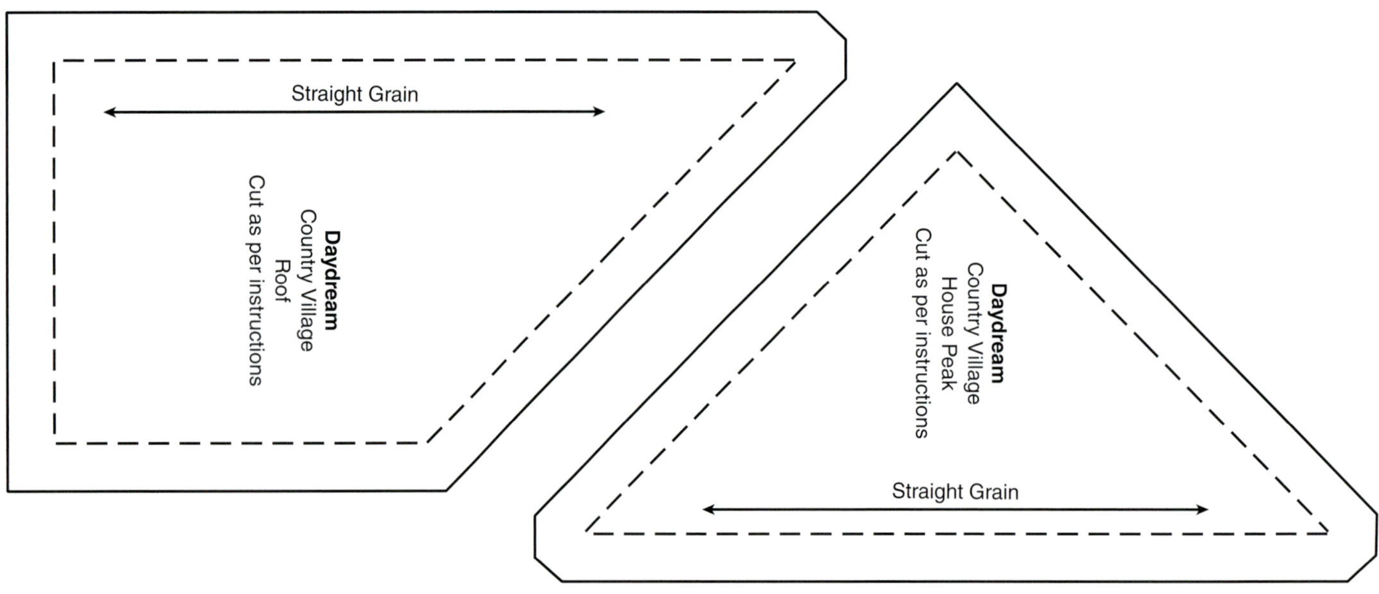

PARTIAL SEAMS

Use partial seaming to join a variety of unevenly placed pieces in a block or unevenly placed blocks or sections in a quilt.

1. Lay out the block pieces or quilt sections around the center piece or block as shown in Figure A.

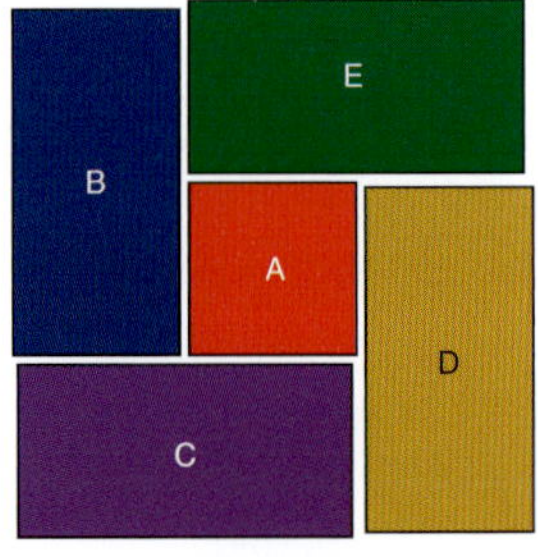

Figure A

2. Referring to Figure B, stitch A (center square) to B (first section) beginning approximately 2" from the bottom corner of A. Finger-press A away from B.

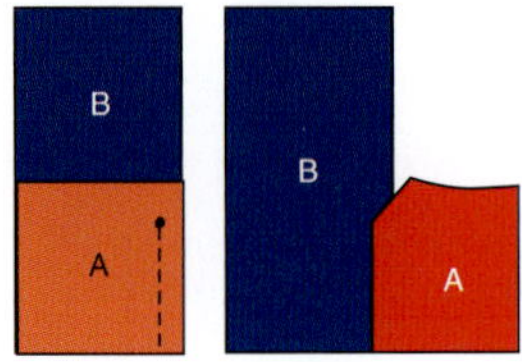

Figure B

3. Working counterclockwise, join C (second section) to the A-B unit as shown in Figure C, stitching the entire length of the seam. Press seam toward C.

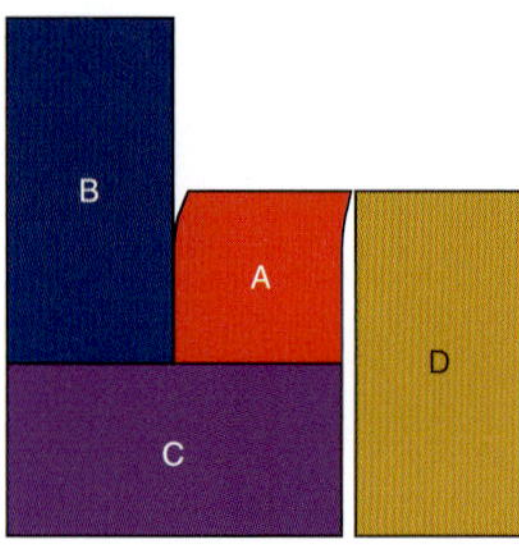

Figure C

4. Match and join D (third section) to A-C edge referring again to Figure C, completing the entire length of the seam. Press seam toward D.

5. Join E (fourth section) to the A-D edge, again completing the entire length of the seam, as shown in Figure D. Be sure to keep B (first section) out of the way when stitching.

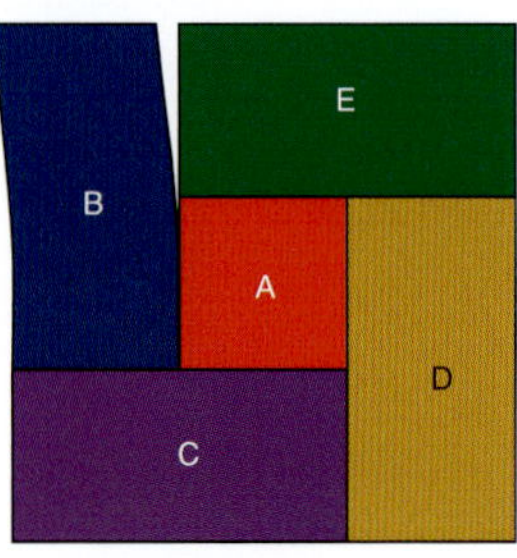

Figure D

6. Complete the assembly by finishing the A-B seam that was partially sewn in step 2. Fold over C and match the B edge to the A-E edge. Lower the machine needle at the end of the A-B seam, backstitch to secure and complete the A-B seam as shown in red in Figure E. Press seam toward B, completing the block or quilt section (Figure F). ●

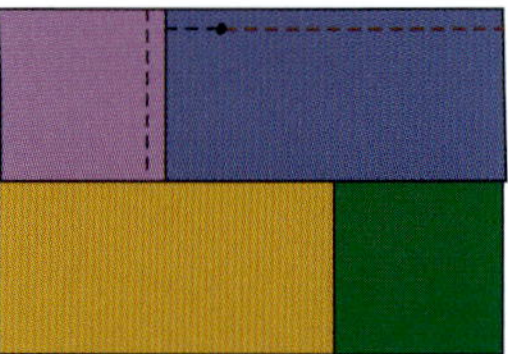
Figure E

Figure F

Cutting

From blue print #4 cut:
- 32 (1½" x WOF) strips

From gray print #5 cut:
- 8 (4½" x WOF) strips
- 16 (1½" x WOF) strips

From yellow print #2 cut:
- 20 (3½") BB squares

From multicolored stripe cut:
- 9 (2½" x WOF) binding strips

Completing the Sashing Rows

1. Gather the blue print #4 (1½"-wide) strips and gray print #5 (1½"-wide) strips. Stitch a blue print #4 strip to opposite long sides of a gray print #5 strip to make a strip set as shown in Figure 1. Make 16. Cut each strip set into two 3½" x 16½" sashing strips. Cut 31 total sashing strips.

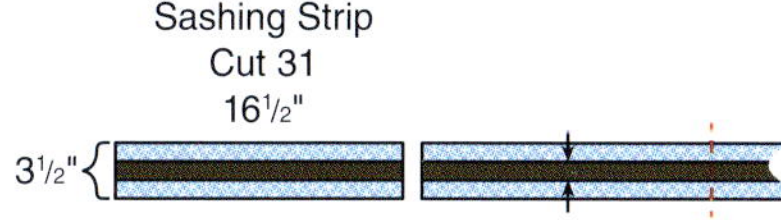

Figure 1

2. Stitch together four BB squares and three sashing strips to make a sashing row as shown in Figure 2. Make five.

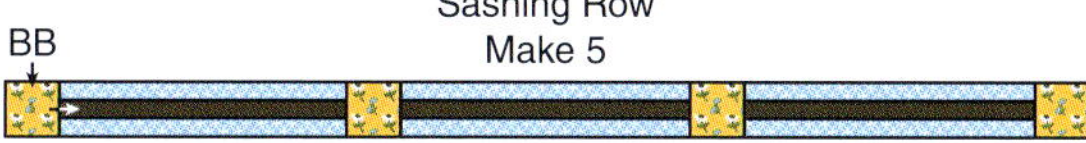

Figure 2

Completing the Quilt

1. Referring to the Assembly Diagram, arrange and sew blocks and sashing strips into four block rows. Place a sashing row between each block row and at the top and bottom. Sew block rows and sashing rows together to complete the quilt center. Press.

CHAPTER 13

Strip Piecing

Sashing Rows & Completing the Quilt

Learn strip piecing and cutting strip set segments.

2. Stitch the 4½"-wide gray print #5 strips together short ends to short ends and subcut into 2 (4½" x 79½") CC and 2 (4½" x 68½") DD border strips. Stitch one CC strip to each side of the quilt center. Press, then stitch one DD strip to the top and bottom. Press.

3. Layer, baste, quilt as desired and bind referring to Quilting Basics.

Daydream Sampler
Assembly Diagram 68" x 87"

Color Your Way

This version of Daydream was pieced by Palmer Bixler using the Lucky in Love Bali Batiks collection from Hoffman California-International Fabrics. Quilted by Karen Somer of Spoolin' Around.

Color Your Way

It's amazing how color choices change up a quilt! The beautiful blues of the Silver Jubilee fabric collection by Maywood Studio are reminiscent of vintage blue-and-white china patterns and transform this quilt into a sophisticated beauty.

Irish Puzzle

In this striking blue version of Daydream called Silver Jubilee, the Country Village block was replaced by the Irish Puzzle block. A kit for Silver Jubilee is available for a limited time at AnniesCraftStore.com.

Design by Carolyn Beam
Quilted by Masterpiece Quilting

Skill Level

Confident Beginner

Finished Size

Block Size: 16" x 16"

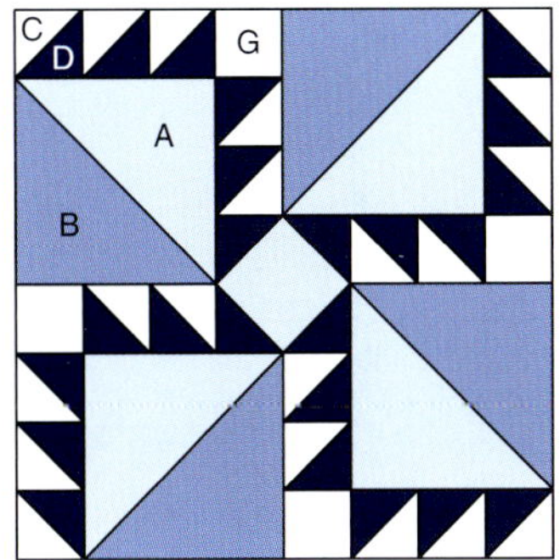

Irish Puzzle
Square block to 16" x 16"
Make 1

Materials

- 1 fat eighth of Fabric 1
- 1 fat eighth of Fabric 2
- 1 fat quarter of Fabric 3
- 1 fat quarter of Fabric 4

Project Notes

Read all instructions before beginning this project.

Stitch right sides together using a ¼" seam allowance unless otherwise specified.

Materials and cutting lists assume 40" of usable fabric width for yardage and 20" for fat quarters and fat eighths.

WOF – width of fabric
HST – half-square triangle ⧄
QST – quarter-square triangle ⊠

Cutting

Refer to the fabric swatches given below.

From Fabric 1 cut:

- 2 (7") B squares

From Fabric 2 cut:

- 2 (7") A squares
- 1 (4½") E square

From Fabric 3 cut:

- 10 (3") D squares
- 4 (2½") F squares

From Fabric 4 cut:

- 10 (3") C squares
- 4 (2½") G squares

Fabric 1

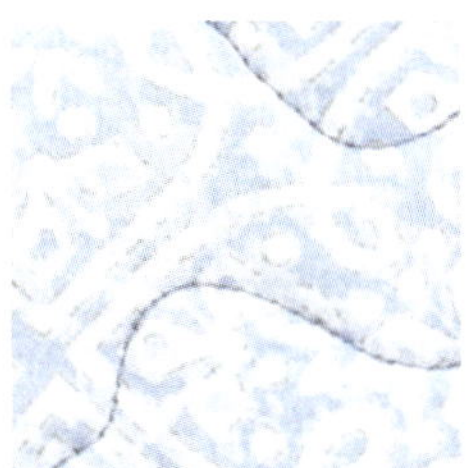
Fabric 2

Fabric 3

Fabric 4

Completing the Block

1. Refer to Half-Square Triangles on page 13 and use A squares and B squares to make four A-B HST units as shown in Figure 1. Trim units to 6½" square, keeping diagonal seam centered.

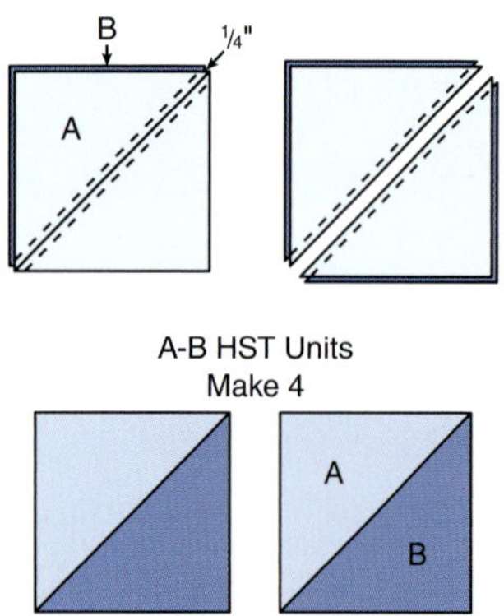

Figure 1

2. In the same manner, use C squares and D squares to make 20 C-D HST units as shown in Figure 2. Trim units to 2½" square, keeping diagonal seam centered.

Figure 2

3. Refer to Sew & Flip Corners on page 7 and sew F squares to the corners of the E square to make the block center unit as shown in Figure 3.

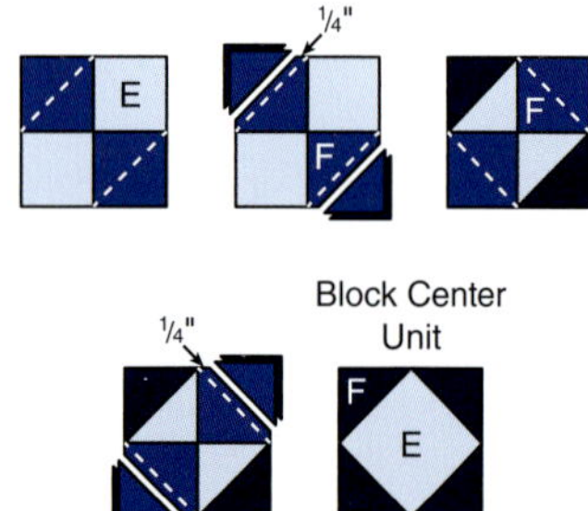

Figure 3

4. Referring to Figure 4 and noting orientation of the units, stitch three C-D HST units together and stitch to the top of an A-B unit. Stitch one G square and two C-D units together and stitch to the bottom of an A-B unit to make a corner unit. Make four corner units.

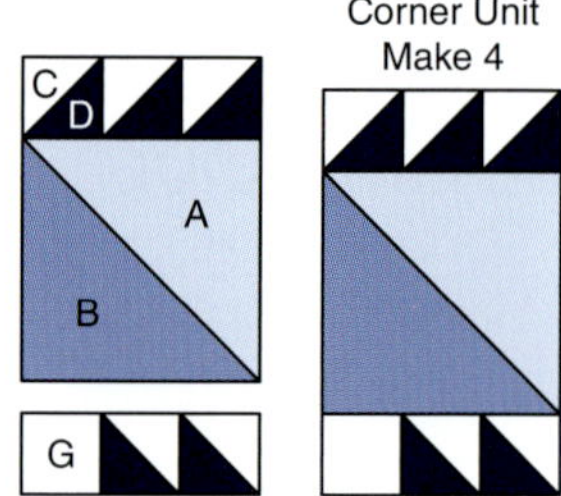

Figure 4

5. Referring to Partial Seams on page 28 and Figure 5, stitch a corner unit to the left side of the block center unit with a partial seam, starting the stitching halfway down the block center unit. Working counterclockwise, add corner units to the bottom, right side and the top of the block center unit. Complete the first seam to complete the Irish Puzzle block. ●

Figure 5

Square & Star Pillow

Add a couple borders to one block for a decorative pillow.

Designed & Quilted by Carolyn Beam

Skill Level
Confident Beginner

Finished Sizes
Pillow Size: 22" x 22"
Block Size: 16" x 16"
Number of Blocks: 1

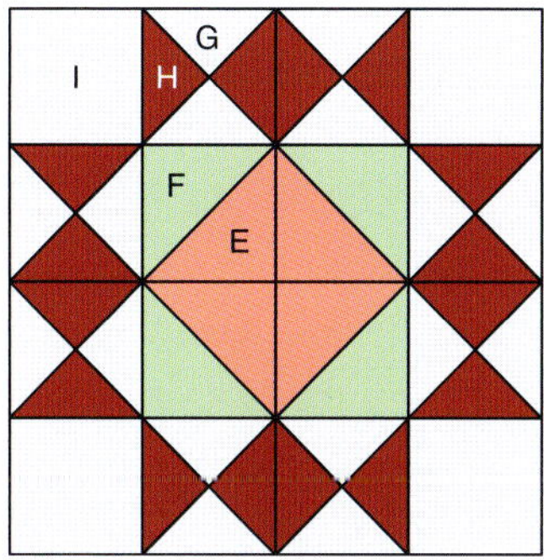

Square & Star
16" x 16" Finished Block
Make 1

Materials
- 1 fat quarter light peach print*
- 1 fat eighth light green small floral print*
- 1 fat quarter white print*
- 1 fat quarter dark peach print*
- ⅝ yard light green large floral print*
- ¾ yard backing fabric*
- 26" x 26" batting*
- 26" x 26" square of muslin
- 22" x 22" pillow form
- Thread*
- Basic sewing tools and supplies

**Fabrics from the Strawberry Lemonade collection by Sherri & Chelsi for Moda Fabrics; Warm & Natural batting from The Warm Company; 50 wt. thread from Aurifil used to make sample.*

Project Notes
Read all instructions before beginning this project.

Stitch right sides together using a ¼" seam allowance unless otherwise specified.

Materials and cutting lists assume 40" of usable fabric width for yardage and 20" for fat quarters and fat eighths.

WOF – width of fabric
HST – half-square triangle ⧄
QST – quarter-square triangle ⊠

Cutting

From light peach cut:

- 2 (5") E squares
- 2 (1½" x 16½") J border strips
- 2 (1½" x 18½") K border strips

From light green small floral print cut:

- 2 (5") F squares

From white print cut:

- 4 (5½") G squares
- 4 (4½") I squares

From dark peach print cut:

- 4 (5½") H squares

From light green large floral print cut:

- 2 (2½" x 18½") L border strips
- 2 (2½" x 22½") M border strips
- 3 (2½" x WOF) binding strips

From backing fabric cut:

- 2 (13½" x 22½") N rectangles

Completing the Pillow Top

1. Referring to Half-Square Triangles on page 13, use E squares and F squares to make four E-F units as shown in Figure 1. Trim each unit to 4½" square, keeping seam centered.

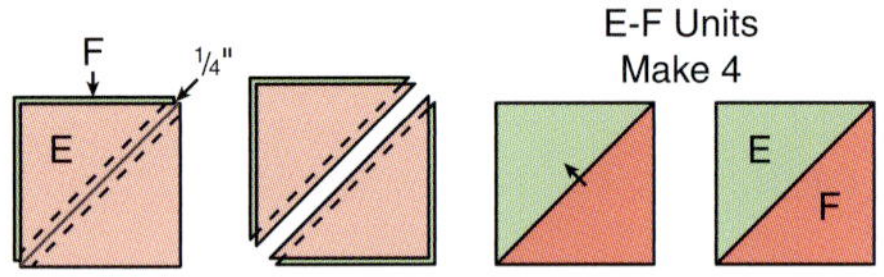

Figure 1

2. In the same manner, make eight G-H units as shown in Figure 2.

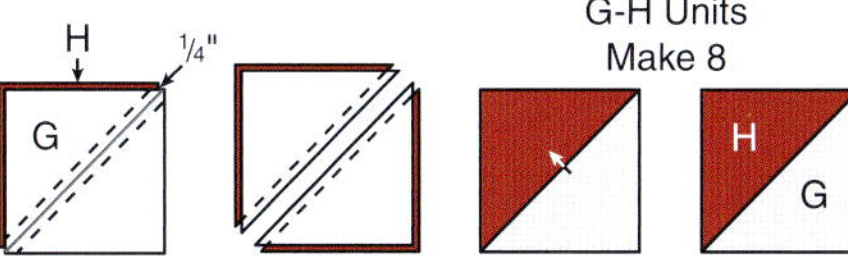

Figure 2

3. Referring to Quarter-Square Triangles on page 15, make eight G-H QST units from step 2 G-H units as shown in Figure 3. Trim QST units to 4½", keeping center point centered.

Figure 3

4. Referring to the Square & Star block diagram, arrange the step 1 and step 3 units along with the I squares in four rows. Stitch the units and squares into rows; sew the rows together to complete the Square & Star block.

5. Add the border strips in alphabetical order to complete the pillow top.

Completing the Pillow

1. Layer and baste together the pillow top, batting and muslin. Quilt as desired. The pillow was quilted with an overall meander. Trim batting and muslin even with the pillow top.

2. Press and sew a double ¼" hem on one long side of each of the N rectangles.

3. Layer the pillow front, right side down, with the two N rectangles right side up and raw edges even as shown in Figure 4. The hemmed edges of the backing rectangles overlap in the center. Stitch around the outside edge.

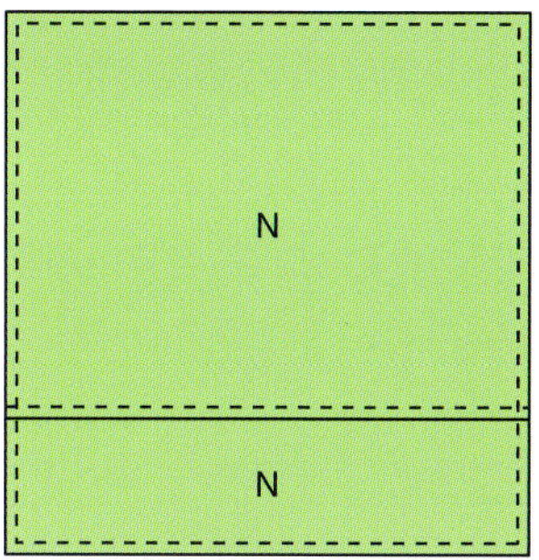

Figure 4

4. Bind the edges of the pillow cover, referring to Quilting Basics, to complete the pillow cover.

5. Insert the pillow form through the opening in the back. ●

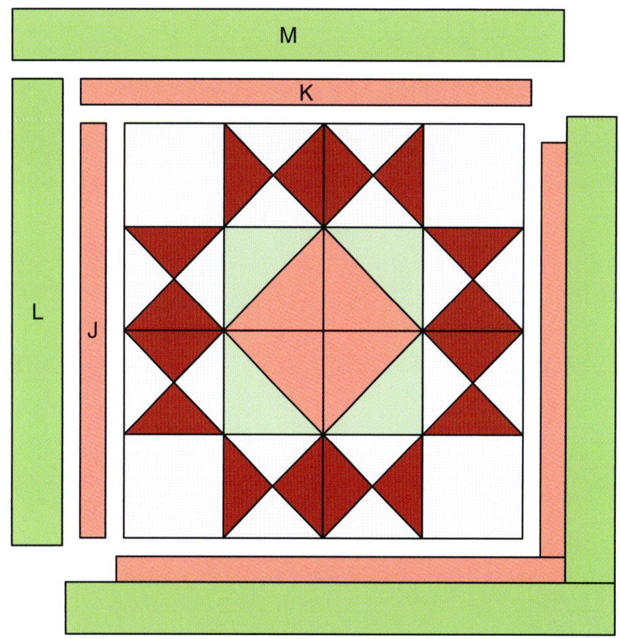

Square & Star Pillow
Assembly Diagram 22" x 22"

Crosses & Losses Quilt

One block in a variety of fabrics makes a lovely throw-size quilt.

Design by Carolyn Beam
Quilted by Cara Cansler of Sew Colorado Quilting

Skill Level

Confident Beginner

Finished Sizes

Quilt Size: 60" x 60"

Block Size: 16" x 16"

Number of Blocks: 9

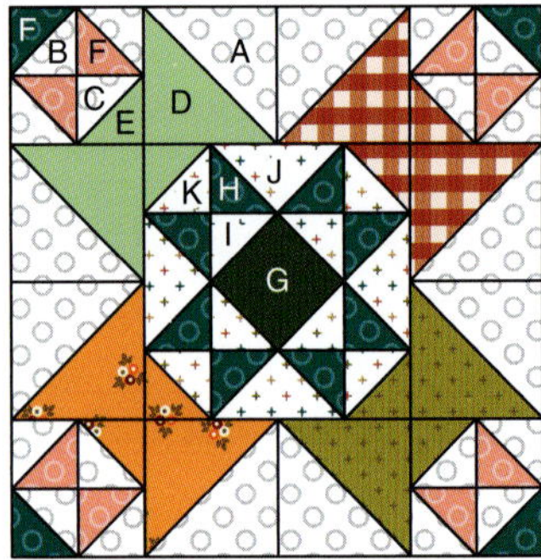

Crosses & Losses
16" x 16" Finished Block
Make 9

Project Notes

Read all instructions before beginning this project.

Stitch right sides together using a ¼" seam allowance unless otherwise specified.

Materials and cutting lists assume 40" of usable fabric width for yardage.

WOF – width of fabric
HST – half-square triangle
QST – quarter-square triangle

Materials

- 1½ yards white print #1*
- 25 precut (10") squares assorted prints*
- 1¾ yards dark teal print*
- ⅞ yard white print #2*
- 1 yard green floral*
- 4⅛ yards backing*
- 68" x 68" batting*
- Thread*
- Basic sewing tools and supplies

**Fabrics from the Strawberry Lemonade collection by Sherri & Chelsi for Moda Fabrics; Hobbs Tuscany Supreme 100% Unbleached Cotton batting; 50 wt. thread from Aurifil used to make sample.*

Cutting

From white print #1 cut:

- 36 (5") A squares
- 54 (3") B squares
- 18 (2⅞") C squares, then cut once diagonally

From each of 18 (10") assorted squares cut:

- 2 (5") D squares (36 total)
- 2 (2⅞") E squares (36 total), then cut once diagonally

From each of 4 (10") squares cut:

- 8 (3") F squares (32 total)

From 1 (10") square cut:

- 4 (3") F squares
- 1 (4½") G square

From each of 2 (10") squares cut:

- 4 (4½") G squares (8 total)

From dark teal print cut:

- 4 (3½") N squares
- 18 (3") F squares
- 36 (2⅞") H squares
- 12 (1½" x WOF) strips
- 7 (2½" x WOF) binding strips

From white print #2 cut:

- 9 (5¼") J squares
- 18 (2⅞") K squares, then cut once diagonally
- 36 (2½") I squares

From green floral cut:

- 4 (3½") L squares
- 8 (3½" x WOF) M border strips. Stitch short ends to short ends and subcut:
  4 (3½" x 54½") M border strips
- 6 (1½" x WOF) strips

Completing the Blocks

1. Referring to Half-Square Triangles on page 13, use A squares and D squares to make 72 A-D units as shown in Figure 1. Trim units to 4½", keeping diagonal seam centered.

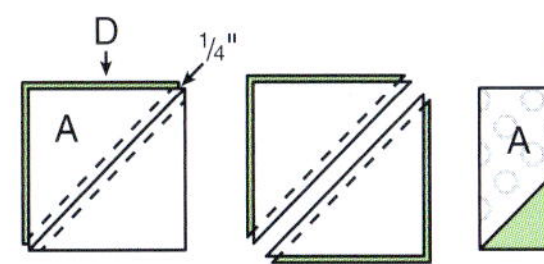

Figure 1

2. Repeat using the B squares and assorted and dark teal print F squares to make 72 assorted B-F units and 36 dark teal B-F units as shown in Figure 2. Trim units to 2½", keeping diagonal seam centered.

Figure 2

3. Refer to Sew & Flip Corners on page 7 and sew I squares to corners of a G square as shown in Figure 3 to make nine square-in-a-square units.

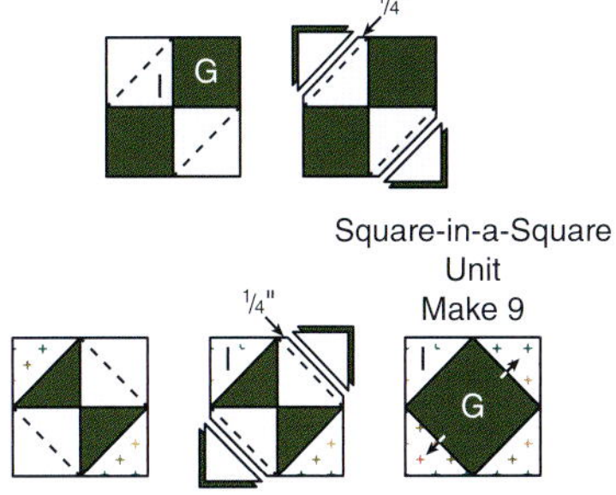

Figure 3

4. Refer to Four-at-a-Time Flying Geese on page 19 and make 36 flying geese using the H and J squares as shown in Figure 4.

Figure 4

5. For each block gather the following:

- 4 sets of two matching A-D units
- 4 sets of two matching E triangles
- 4 dark teal B-F units
- 8 matching assorted B-F units
- 4 C triangles
- 4 K triangles
- 4 flying geese
- 1 square-in-a-square unit

6. Arrange one dark teal B-F unit, two assorted B-F units and one each C and E triangle. Sew the C and E triangles together. Arrange the units as shown in Figure 5. Sew the units into rows; sew the rows together to make a corner unit. Repeat to make four corner units.

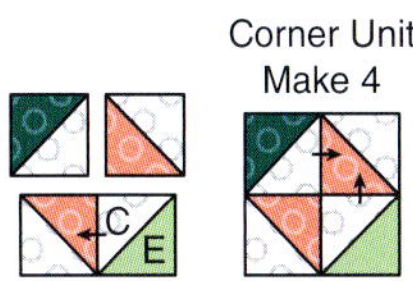

Figure 5

7. Sew the K triangles to the remaining E triangles. Arrange the four E-K units, four flying geese and one square-in-a-square in three rows as shown in Figure 6. Stitch the units into rows; sew the rows together to make the center unit.

Figure 6

8. Refer to the block diagram to arrange the A-D units, corner units and center unit into rows, paying close attention to color placement. Stitch the units together into rows; sew the rows together to complete a Crosses & Losses block. Repeat steps 5–8 to make nine blocks.

Completing the Sashing Rows

1. Gather the dark teal print 1½"-wide strips and green floral 1½"-wide strips. Stitch a dark teal print strip to opposite sides of a green floral strip to make a strip set as shown in Figure 7. Make six. Cut each strip set into two 3½" x 16½" sashing strips. Cut 12 total sashing strips.

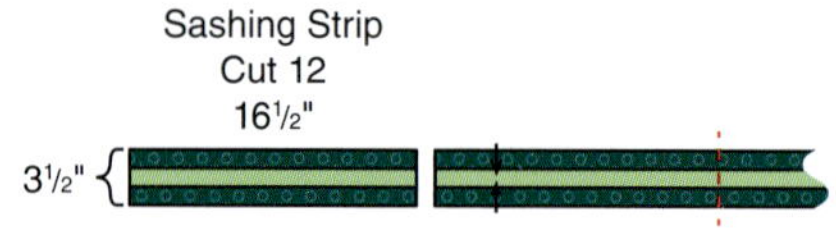

Figure 7

2. Stitch together two L squares and three sashing strips to make a sashing row as shown in Figure 8. Make two.

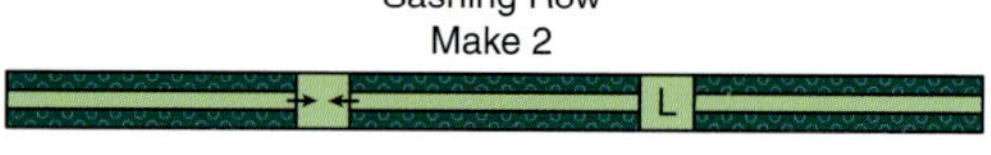

Figure 8

Completing the Quilt

1. Referring to the Assembly Diagram, arrange and sew blocks and sashing strips into three rows. Place a sashing row between each block row. Sew block rows and sashing rows together to complete the quilt center. Press.

2. Stitch one M strip to opposite sides of the quilt center. Press. Sew an N square to each end of the remaining M strips and sew to the top and bottom to complete the quilt center.

3. Layer, baste, quilt as desired and bind referring to Quilting Basics. The photographed quilt was quilted with a floral and vine design. ●

Crosses & Losses
Assembly Diagram 60" x 60"

Quilting Basics

The following is a reference guide. For more information, consult a comprehensive quilting book.

ALWAYS:

- Read through the entire pattern before you begin your project.
- Purchase high-quality, 100 percent cotton fabrics.
- When considering prewashing, do so with ALL of the fabrics being used.
- Use ¼" seam allowance for all stitching unless otherwise instructed.
- Use a short-to-medium stitch length (2.0–2.2).
- Make sure your seams are accurate.

QUILTING TOOLS & SUPPLIES

- Rotary cutter and mat
- Rotary cutting rulers
- Scissors for paper and fabric
- Marking tools
- Sewing machine
- Sewing machine feet:
  - ¼" seaming foot (optional for piecing)
  - Walking or even-feed foot (for piecing or quilting)
  - Darning or free-motion foot (for free-motion quilting)
- Thread
- Straight pins
- Seam ripper
- Iron and ironing surface
- Needles for sewing and/or quilting
- Safety pins or spray baste for basting

BASIC TECHNIQUES

Appliqué

Fusible Appliqué

All templates in *Quilter's World* are reversed for use with this technique.

1. Trace the specified number of templates ¼" apart onto the paper side of paper-backed fusible web. Cut apart the templates, leaving a margin around each, and fuse to the wrong side of the fabric following fusible web manufacturer's instructions.

2. Cut the appliqué pieces out on the traced lines, remove paper backing and apply as instructed in the pattern using the manufacturer's instructions for the fusible web.

3. Finish appliqué raw edges with a straight, satin, blanket, zigzag or blind-hem machine stitch with matching or invisible thread.

Turned-Edge Appliqué

1. Trace the printed reversed templates onto template plastic. Flip the template over and mark as the right side.

2. Position the template, right side up, on the right side of fabric and lightly trace, spacing shapes ½" apart. Cut apart, leaving a $^{3}/_{16}$" to ¼" margin around the traced lines.

3. Clip curves and finger-press edges to the wrong side just inside the traced line.

4. Referring to the appliqué motif, pin or baste appliqué shapes to the background.

5. Hand-stitch shapes in place using a blind stitch and thread to match or machine-stitch using a short blind hemstitch and either matching or invisible thread.

Borders

Most *Quilter's World* patterns give an exact size to cut borders. Check those sizes by comparing them to the horizontal and vertical center measurements of your quilt top.

Straight Borders

1. Mark the centers of the side borders and quilt top sides.

2. Stitch side borders to left and right sides of the quilt top with right sides together and matching raw edges and center marks using a ¼" seam. Press seams toward borders.

3. Repeat with top and bottom borders.

Mitered Borders

1. Add at least twice the border width to the border lengths instructed to cut.

2. Center and sew the side borders to the quilt, beginning and ending stitching ¼" from the quilt corner and backstitching (Figure 1). Repeat with the top and bottom borders.

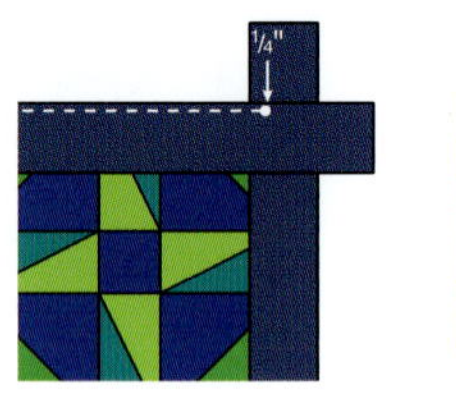

Figure 1

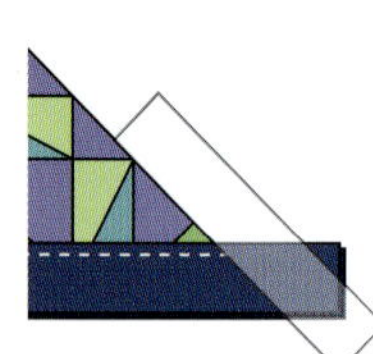
Figure 2

3. Fold and pin quilt right sides together at a 45-degree angle on one corner, matching border edges (Figure 2). Place a straightedge along the fold and lightly mark a line across the border ends.

4. Starting at the ¼" mark where sewing on the border starts and stops, stitch along the line, backstitching to secure. Trim seam to ¼" and press open (Figure 3).

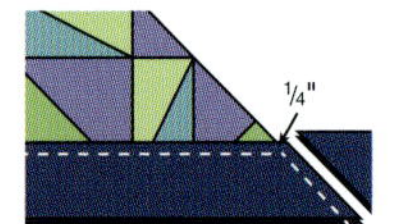

Figure 3

Quilt Backing & Batting

Cut your backing and batting 8" larger than the finished quilt-top size and 4" larger for quilts smaller than 50" square. ***Note:*** *Check with longarm quilter about their requirements, if applicable. For baby quilts not going to a longarm quilter 4"–6" overall may be sufficient.* If preparing the backing from standard-width fabrics, remove the selvages and sew two or three lengths together; press seams open. If using 108"-wide fabric, trim to size on the straight grain of the fabric. Prepare batting the same size as your backing.

Quilting

1. Press quilt top on both sides and trim all loose threads. ***Note:*** *If you are sending your quilt to a longarm quilter, contact them for specifics about preparing your quilt for quilting.*

2. Mark quilting design on quilt top. Make a quilt sandwich by layering the backing right side down, batting and quilt top centered right side up on flat surface and smooth out. Baste layers together using pins, thread basting or spray basting to hold. ***Note:*** *Tape or pin backing to surface to hold taut while layering and avoid puckers.*

3. Quilt as desired by hand or machine. Remove pins or basting as you quilt.

4. Trim batting and backing edges even with raw edges of quilt top.

Binding the Quilt

1. Join binding strips on short ends with diagonal seams to make one long strip; trim seams to ¼" and press seams open (Figure 4).

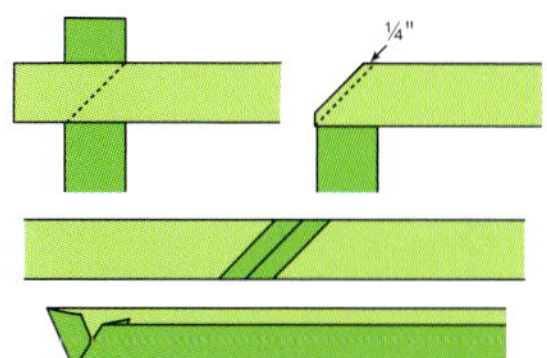

Figure 4

2. Fold ½" of one short end to wrong side and press. Fold the binding strip in half with wrong sides together along length, again referring to Figure 4; press.

3. Starting about 3" from the folded short end, sew binding to quilt top edges, matching raw edges and using a ¼" seam. Stop stitching ¼" from corner and backstitch (Figure 5).

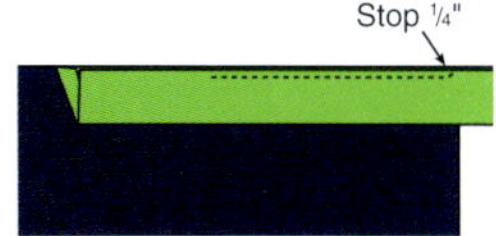

Figure 5

4. Fold binding up at a 45-degree angle to seam and then down even with quilt edges, forming a pleat at corner (Figure 6).

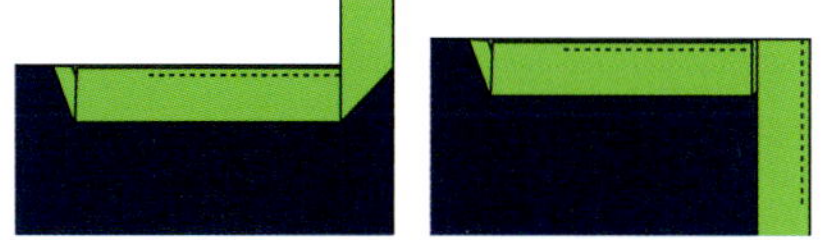

Figure 6

5. Resume stitching from corner edge as shown in Figure 6, down quilt side, backstitching ¼" from next corner. Repeat, mitering all corners, stitching to within 3" of starting point.

6. Trim binding, leaving enough length to tuck inside starting end and complete stitching (Figure 7).

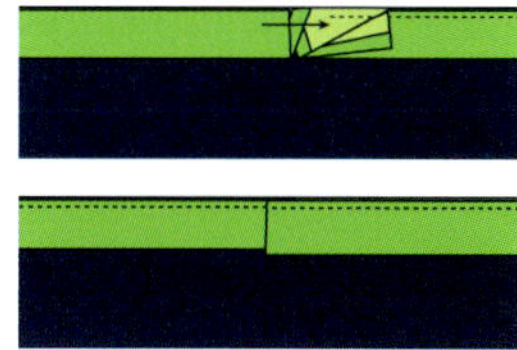

Figure 7

7. If stitching binding by hand, machine-sew binding to the front of the quilt and fold to the back before stitching. If stitching by machine, machine-sew binding to back of the quilt and fold to the front before stitching.

QUILTING TERMS

- **Appliqué:** Adding fabric motifs to a background fabric by hand or machine (see Appliqué section of Basic Techniques).
- **Basting:** Temporarily securing layers of quilting materials together with safety pins, thread or a temporary spray adhesive in preparation for quilting the layers.
- **Batting:** An insulating material made in a variety of fibers that is used between the quilt top and back to provide extra warmth and loft.
- **Binding:** A finishing strip of fabric sewn to the outer raw edges of a quilt to cover them.

  Straight-grain binding strips, cut on the crosswise straight grain of the fabric, are commonly used.

  Bias binding strips are cut at a 45-degree angle to the straight grain of the fabric. They are used when binding is being added to curved edges or as a design choice (see Straight & Bias Grain Lines illustration on next page).
- **Block:** The basic quilting unit that is often repeated to complete the quilt's design composition. Blocks can be pieced, appliquéd or solid and are usually square or rectangular in shape.

- **Border:** The frame of a quilt's central design used to visually complete the design and give the eye a place to rest.
- **Fabric Grain:** The fibers that run either parallel (lengthwise grain) or perpendicular (crosswise grain) to the fabric selvage are straight grain.

  Bias is any diagonal line between the lengthwise or crosswise grain. At these angles the fabric is less stable and stretches easily. The true bias of a woven fabric is a 45-degree angle between the lengthwise and crosswise grain lines.

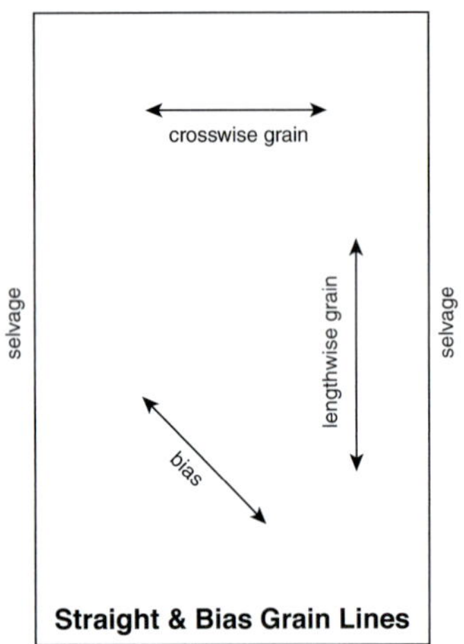

Straight & Bias Grain Lines

- **Mitered Corners:** Matching borders or turning bindings at a 45-degree angle at corners.
- **Patchwork:** A general term for the completed blocks or quilts that are made from smaller shapes sewn together.
- **Pattern:** This may refer to the design of a fabric or to the written instructions for a particular quilt design.
- **Piecing:** The act of sewing smaller pieces and/or units of a block or quilt together.

  Paper or foundation piecing is sewing fabric to a paper or cloth foundation in a certain order.

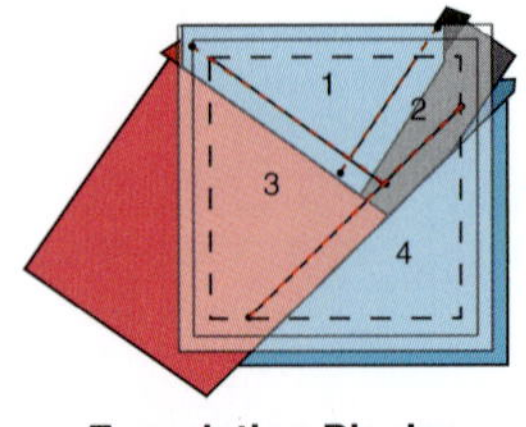

Foundation Piecing

String or chain piecing is sewing pieces together in a continuous string without clipping threads between sections.

String or Chain Piecing

Pressing: Pressing is the process of placing the iron on the fabric, lifting it off the fabric and placing it down in another location to flatten seams or crease fabric without sliding the iron across the fabric.

Quilters do not usually use steam when pressing, since it can easily distort fabric shapes.

Generally, seam allowances are pressed toward the darker fabric in quilting so that they do not show through the lighter fabric.

Seams are pressed in opposite directions where seams are being joined to allow seams to butt against each other and to distribute bulk.

Seams are pressed open when multiple seams come together in one place.

If you have a question about pressing direction, consult a comprehensive quilting guide for guidance.

- **Quilt (noun):** A sandwich of two layers of fabric with a third insulating material between them that is then stitched together with the edges covered or bound.
- **Quilt (verb):** Stitching several layers of fabric materials together with a decorative design. Stippling, crosshatch, channel, in-the-ditch, free-motion, allover and meandering are all terms for quilting designs.

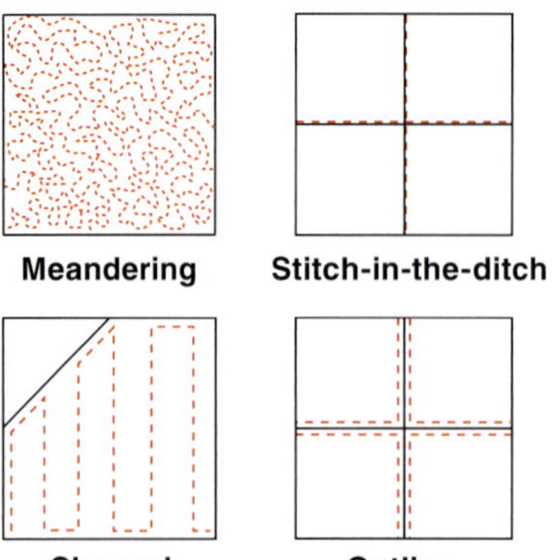

- **Quilt Sandwich:** A layer of insulating material between a quilt's top and back fabric.
- **Rotary Cutting:** Using a rotary cutting blade and straightedge to cut fabric.
- **Sashing:** Strips of fabric sewn between blocks to separate or set off the designs.
- **Subcut:** A second cutting of rotary-cut strips that makes the basic shapes used in block and quilt construction.
- **Template:** A pattern made from a sturdy material which is then used to cut shapes for patchwork and appliqué quilting.

QUILTING SKILL LEVELS

- **Beginner**
  These projects are suitable for a quilter who has been introduced to the basics of cutting, piecing and assembling a quilt top and is working to master these skills. Beginner patterns require the knowledge of how to sandwich, quilt and bind a quilt, but do not require experience with these skills.
- **Confident Beginner**
  These projects are suitable for a quilter who has pieced and assembled several quilt tops and is comfortable with the process. Confident Beginner patterns include more challenging techniques and use at least two different techniques.
- **Intermediate**
  These projects are suitable for a quilter who is comfortable with most quilting techniques and has a good understanding of design, color and the whole process. Intermediate projects involve multiple techniques and may include paper piecing or bias piecing. The projects may allow for fabric selections other that those listed in the pattern.
- **Advanced**
  These projects are challenging designs suitable for a quilter who is willing to try any technique and is able to read, comprehend and complete a pattern. Advanced projects may require selecting fabric suited to the design. ●

Supplies

We would like to thank the following manufacturers who provided materials to make sample projects for this book.

Color Your Way, page 31: Fabrics from the Lucky in Love Bali Batiks collection from Hoffman California-International Fabrics.

Color Your Way, page 32: Fabrics from the Silver Jubilee fabric collection by Maywood Studio.

Square & Star Pillow, page 35: Fabrics from the Strawberry Lemonade collection by Sherri & Chelsi for Moda Fabrics; Warm & Natural batting from The Warm Company; Aurifil 50 wt. thread.

Crosses & Losses Quilt, page 38: Fabrics from the Strawberry Lemonade collection by Sherri & Chelsi for Moda Fabrics; Hobbs Tuscany Supreme 100% Unbleached Cotton batting; Aurifil 50 wt. thread.

Special Thanks

Please join us in thanking the talented quilters whose work is featured in this collection.

Daydream Sampler, 2
Quilted by Donna Smith

Irish Puzzle, 33
Quilted by Masterpiece Quilting

Square & Star Pillow, 35
Quilted by Carolyn Beam

Crosses & Losses Quilt, 38
Quilted by Cara Cansler of Sew Colorado Quilting

Annie's® Published by Annie's, 306 East Parr Road, Berne, IN 46711. Printed in USA.

RETAIL STORES: If you would like to carry this publication or any other Annie's publications, visit AnniesWSL.com.

ISBN: 979-8-89253-387-4

1 2 3 4 5 6 7 8 9